STARTING OVER

HOW TO SURVIVE AND THRIVE AFTER
A REVERSAL OF FORTUNE

STARTING OVER

HOW TO SURVIVE AND THRIVE AFTER A REVERSAL OF FORTUNE

TOM FINI

OTHER PEOPLE'S KNOWLEDGE, LLC
BEDFORD, NEW HAMPSHIRE

Book Cover/Interior/eBook Design by The Book Cover Whisperer: ProfessionalBookCoverDesign.com

Registration Number TXu 2-169-658

978-1-7348313-1-3 Paperback
978-1-7348313-0-6 Hardcover
978-1-7348313-2-0 eBook
978-1-7348313-3-7 Audio Book

Printed in the U.S.A.

FIRST EDITION

To my wife, Carol, my biggest fan, who allowed me to pursue my dreams, often at the expense of her own; to my children and grandchildren, who are my greatest source of inspiration; and to my extended family and friends, who were my bridge back to sanity when all seemed to be lost.

CONTENTS

INTRODUCTION

ONE OF THE MORE UNFORTUNATE facts of life is that highly successful men and women can mismanage their careers, finances, or relationships and struggle for years, even decades, trying to recover. Famous actors, athletes, lawyers, doctors, musicians, and business leaders from all walks of life are not immune to a potential reversal of fortune, and once in this state, many experience mental and emotional stress that can lead to physical illness. This turn of events is even more devastating for those who are over 50 years old, a time of life when rebuilding a career or relationship or recovering from a financial failure can seem nearly impossible.

Think of the failures of some of America's largest corporations, such as General Motors, Chrysler, Polaroid, American Airlines, and Eastman Kodak. As Jim Pohlad, turnaround specialist, points out, "Nothing is so successful that it can't be mismanaged. If these large corporations can be mismanaged with millions of dollars and unlimited consultants available to them, it is certainly possible to mismanage your own affairs."

Elton John, Willie Nelson, Kim Basinger, Nicholas Cage, Mike Tyson, Walt Disney, Cyndi Lauper, and yes, Presidents Donald Trump, Thomas Jefferson, and Abraham Lincoln all filed for bankruptcy. There are thousands of other famous and not so famous individuals who have gone from success to failure for one reason or another.

During our time together, we will examine the causes of failure and what needs to be done to fully recover, particularly if you are in the latter part of your life. It will not be easy. It will require a thorough examination of what caused the failure in the first place, so you will not repeat that behavior in the future and end up with the same unsatisfactory results. It will require developing new attitudes and remembering what made you a success the first time around. If success has eluded you, this information will provide a platform for you to achieve what you dreamed about but believed it was too late to accomplish.

All of the aforementioned corporations and individuals found their way back to success. We will identify the process they used so that you can use it as a roadmap for your own return to success. For some, that may mean millions of dollars; for others, considerably less. For some, it's a return to a status they once had, and for others, it's a return to their definition of the good life. For all, it will require understanding the Essential Common Denominators of Success. In simple terms, this book will show you how to get your "groove" back at any age, but especially if you're over 50. Aging should be looked at as a transition, not an ending.

In 1949, Konrad Adenauer became the first chancellor

of Germany after World War II. He was 73 when he was elected and governed Germany for 14 years. He oversaw the reconstruction of that country from a defeated and ruined country to a nation surpassed only by the U.S. in the production of goods and services. Adenauer governed Germany longer than Hitler.

Patrick Gass was 91 years old when he volunteered to serve for the Union Army in the Civil War. Fifty-eight years earlier, he had been a member of the Lewis and Clark expedition. Age certainly didn't stop him from continuing to explore life.

Ray Kroc didn't own his first McDonald's until he was over 50 and turned it into the largest fast-food concept in the world. Colonel Sanders was 66 when he opened his first KFC.

Nola (Hill) Ochs became a Guinness World Record holder as the world's oldest college graduate. The 95-year-old graduated from Fort Hays State University in Kansas alongside her granddaughter, who was 21 at the time. Nola continued studies and received her master's degree at age 98.

George Burns, the comedian and actor, wrote eight books starting in his late 70s, and all of them were bestsellers. He won an Academy Award at age 79 and continued to make movies into his 90s.

Harry Bernstein spent a lifetime writing in obscurity but finally achieved fame at age 96 for his bestselling memoir about Alzheimer's, *The Invisible Wall: A Love Story That Broke Barriers.*

Donald Trump and Hillary Clinton, presidential candidates in the 2016 election, were 70 and 69 years old, respectively. Each ran such a vigorous campaign that even a 30-something would have had a difficult time keeping up with their pace.

I am not only the author of this book about the road back to success but someone who traveled that road after age 50. The most important insight I want you to take away from reading what I have to say is that it's not over, even if you are starting over over 50. Age is truly a state of mind. If you are still able to cast a shadow, you can improve your life. Don't look back—we're not going that way. The past is fixed and cannot be changed. We will be concerned only with the present and the plans you will develop to create a new role for yourself in the future. Because I didn't have the roadmap I'll be sharing with you, I struggled unnecessarily for more than three years. The Essential Common Denominators of Success are principles that are universal and relevant to everyone. They will be a reliable guide to the success and happiness you desire. As cliché as it may sound, this truly is the first day of the rest of your exciting life: *"Rejoice and be glad in it!"*

STARTING
OVER

FACTORY TOWN

"I was born and raised in a little factory town,
Where the wheels in the mills, they all
turned round and round,
From inside those walls, you never heard
the sound, Of the gentle rain, falling on
the ground." —George Tocci

LEOMINSTER, MASSACHUSETTS WAS known as the pioneer plastic city. I was born the year after the war ended, and Americans were very positive about their future, as they should have been. The world was at peace, and the "Greatest Generation" had just completed an impossible mission successfully. Nothing was impossible anymore.

One of the challenges for the millions of returning soldiers was to determine what career path they would follow. The GI bill allowed most of them the opportunity to attend college or trade school and assimilate back into society with an advanced education and a promising future in the country they had just risked their lives to preserve. Expectations were at an all-time high.

My father was one of 11 children from an Italian immigrant family. Like many other returning fighters, he had to start over. After high school, he had taken a job as an advertising salesman for the *Boston Herald*. The war interrupted that career, just as it had interrupted the career of almost every other able-bodied person over the age of 18. Upon returning home, he went to work as a sales representative for a local manufacturer of combs, charms, and other toys made from plastic. In those days, before the world recognized the amazing qualities and potential uses of this versatile material, plastics were mostly relegated to such inexpensive trinkets. My father traveled to New York City often to meet with buyers from department stores who purchased the products manufactured by his firm. Things were good in the Fini family. We were living in a new, temporary housing development, which later became known as "the project." Similar housing units were constructed in many areas of the country to accommodate returning veterans until they could resettle into more permanent homes.

Every year or two, another member joined our family. Before my mother was through having babies, we had grown to seven kids. My father's 10 siblings were also very active in the baby-making department. It wasn't long before there were more than 40 first cousins for us to play with.

My grandfather and grandmother owned a small house about a mile from the center of town where they had raised their 11 children. It provided a common meeting place for all the new and old family members. It was a storybook escape, filled with love and understanding for all of us. It didn't matter what was taking place in your life outside those walls; this was a safe refuge. You were protected there. My grandparents made everyone feel very special and unique. In fact, it wasn't until years later, at my grandmother's funeral, that I learned that I was not her only favorite grandchild. She had told every one of my cousins that they were her favorite, too, but to keep it a secret between them. She truly loved all of us with the same intensity. You could see it in her eyes at every encounter. When she hugged you, it was hard to let go.

Like my father, my aunts and uncles were also optimistic about their future in America. One uncle was lost in the war, but the 10 remaining children were determined to make their mark in the world. Some were content to do it where they grew up and stayed nearby, while others opted for a more adventurous journey to other parts of the country.

I'm making note of these different facts because they play an essential role in starting out or starting over. Everyone's life has a foundation. That foundation will influence the direction you take as you build above the foundation. The stronger the foundation, the greater the chances of your own personal success. However, even a difficult childhood can have very positive aspects if you recognize the value of the lessons you learned.

Situations can change in a split second. Your entire life can be affected by a single event, occasionally beyond your control. When the phone rang at the Fini residence on a frigid New England night, little did we know that our childhood would never be the same.

"Fire is raging at the factory!" the caller said in a hurried and frantic voice.

I could hear him clearly through the receiver, even though it was against my father's ear.

"Is everyone out of the place?" my father inquired.

"Yes, but the fire is in the warehouse; things are starting to explode; I don't think there's any hope!"

"Is Cy there?" Dad asked.

"His number was busy, so I called you; you need to get here right away Wally."

My father hung up the phone, turned to my mother, and mumbled, "The factory is burning—I have to go."

A few days later, my mother took us to the scene. The place where my father had worked was now a pile of smoldering red bricks. The only identifiable remnant of the structure was the towering circular chimney, now encased in dripping bands of frozen water that resembled the icing on a scalloped birthday cake. The smell of gasified plastic resin permeated the cold air as the firemen continued to hose down the warehouse. Spectators stood behind the red and white cones delineating the safe zone. No one was talking, the view spoke for itself. It was a catastrophic event for our small town and the employees at the facility, including my father. He was now unemployed.

THE ORIGINAL TIN MEN

MY UNCLE SILVIO WAS in town from California at this time. He had moved out West after the war, attempting to find a career in the movie business. Using the stage name Jack Martin, he managed to secure a few small parts in B-rated movies, including a cameo with the Dead-End Kids. Now, searching for a more stable paycheck, he was back home in Massachusetts for a trip down memory lane, hoping something might inspire a new direction. He, my father, and my Uncle Johnny started to discuss possibilities. Uncle Silvio had worked construction, and my father and Uncle Johnny were salesmen. Aluminum siding had just come on the market, and the manufacturers were eager to acquire representatives to sell and install their product. My father decided not to continue his career in plastics and partnered with Uncle Silvio and Uncle Johnny to start National Home and Remodeling Company, a distributor of Alcoa Aluminum siding products.

The company consisted of two salesmen, a set-up man, and two installers—far from the national company the name implied. They were the original tin men in our area.

My mother was adamantly against this venture. Now with five kids and another on the way, the last thing she wanted was the uncertainty of a start-up venture, especially with my Uncle Silvio. He was notorious for organizing parties, with or without holidays, and as of the time he arrived back home, he hadn't made a payment on his yellow Hudson convertible in more than three months. He was hoping that the auto finance company from California wouldn't catch up with him until he could actually afford the car he was driving. Despite the objections of my mother, the business was incorporated, and National Home and Remodeling Company became a reality.

My mother was right about this dubious association. The three partners were really good at what they did—when they worked. A significant amount of their time was invested in gambling at the area race tracks during the day, and my father would spend many of his nights buying drinks for everyone at the neighborhood bars. Needless to say, the family finances and my father's inebriation became a constant battle between my parents. Violent outbursts were commonplace whenever my father was home. Fortunately, he traveled enough that frequent hotel stays were a necessary part of his weekly plan.

Living conditions never improved during the entire

time I lived at home. Every Saturday morning, the bill collectors routinely knocked on our door. Many times we would hide and pretend that we weren't home. My mother didn't have a car in those days, and I'm certain most of the collectors knew we were hiding behind the couch or under the kitchen table. On a good Saturday, my mother would pay everyone $2.00 on our account, just to keep the bread and milk deliveries coming. She frequently said we are all going to end up in the poorhouse someday. I had no idea what the poorhouse was, but if it was worse than living in the project, I reasoned, it must be a pretty horrible place. This was the fractured environment in which my siblings and I started our life's journey.

My Guitar

I WAS A HANDFUL AS A KID. My daily adventures were non-stop—whether it was pretending to be Davy Crockett in the woods, playing sandlot baseball, or making trips to the local dump to rummage for construction materials to build tree forts. Sitting still was not part of my agenda. At times I'm sure the constant cuts, scrapes, bruises, and stitches were overwhelming to my mother. And then there was the day that I lost my grip and parted company with a Tarzan swing we had tied to a giant hillside oak towering above the forest floor below. When I finally stopped rolling down the hill, my collarbone, shoulder, and wrist were severely fractured. Weeks in a full upper-body cast were torture for an active 12-year-old. Within days after the cast finally came off, a failed attempt to catch a badly thrown pass ended in a clash between my elbow and the sidewalk, dislocating the only joint in my left arm not fractured from the earlier event.

In an attempt to find something that might slow me down enough to recover from my injuries, my mother asked me if I would be interested in getting a guitar. She was aware of my friendship with Rocky, a project resident who played guitar in a local country band. With the little money she had, she found a way to buy my first guitar. I'm sure that was not an easy task, considering that just buying groceries was a constant challenge. That guitar changed my life, just as the fire at my father's factory changed his. Not only did it occupy a significant amount of my time, but it also provided an opportunity for accomplishment and satisfaction that I still realize today. With that guitar, I became part of a local teenage band that recorded records and performed in front of many large audiences from Boston to Chicago. It gave me an expanded view of the world and boosted my confidence. That experience evolved into the many successful career pursuits that followed and helped me become wealthy at 40. Unfortunately, all of it was gone before I was 50 years old, and the prospects of starting over at age 50 became a painful reality. Here's what happened.

WORK!!!

MY FIRST REAL JOB EXPERIENCE came after my rock 'n' roll
teen days were over. I was 21, married, and we were expecting our first child when I started to interview for more
traditional employment. My hair was down to my shoulders,
I had no college or job experience, and my only acquired
skills were rhythm guitar and backup vocals. It was a sparse
resume. A help-wanted ad in the Boston Sunday Globe from
an employer seeking sales and service representatives for a
new copier manufacturer caught my attention. One of my
responsibilities during my band days was fixing equipment
and cables whenever the need arose. I called the firm and
scheduled an interview for the service position. Although
the ad specifically read "No experience necessary, will train,"
the branch manager said he needed someone with a background in electronics other than electric guitar amps and
speaker systems.

"How about the sales position you advertised—is that still available?"

"Yes, but we need someone with basic sales skills that we can develop" was his reply.

"How do you know if someone has basic sales skills?"

I could see he was beginning to become a little annoyed with me and wanted me to leave; however, he did respond to the question.

"I can tell from sitting in an interview if someone is a good candidate for a sales position.

For example, your suit looks like it should be worn on stage with your band, and your tie is twice as wide as mine, with a psychedelic pattern that is very distracting. Your hairstyle is not representative of the image we would expect for a person contacting lawyers, accountants, and insurance companies. You're wearing boots, and you seem very nervous instead of relaxed and confident."

I was a little hurt from his assessment, but I persisted.

"I really would like an opportunity to prove myself. It would be easy to change everything you just mentioned. Can you consider hiring me on a trial basis to see if it works out?"

The next 30 seconds were the longest of my life, as he just stared at me. Finally, he said, "I have a territory in Roxbury and Dorchester open. It would be an all-commission position, and you will have to pay your own expenses. The company doesn't reimburse you."

"What kind of training is available?"

"We can have you work with one of our other representatives for a couple of weeks to show you how the process works. After that, you can start developing your assigned territory. We can give you a 90-day evaluation period to see if this is the right situation for both of us."

Sales work was very difficult at first. Only a few customers were interested in our products. We were a competitor to Xerox, and they left very little room for others to make any measurable headway. The territory that my manager assigned me was in a disadvantaged part of Boston. The crime rate was very high in those days, and many of the business owners were not receptive to scheduling appointments with the new kid on the block, especially if it meant spending money on office equipment. Moreover, the best prospects in the district included some of the largest hospitals in Boston. These accounts were 100% controlled by Xerox. My manager told me not to waste time on them because they have a national pricing contract, and we were not competitive. I decided to call on them anyway, just to know what it would be like to meet with a large institution. And besides, I could wear my new suit and shoes and act as if I were an important person coming to meet with the top hospital administrators.

One of the few features our equipment had that Xerox technology had not yet developed was a precision lens that could duplicate a picture with impeccable accuracy. Most users had little or no need to copy pictures; however, on a sales call to Brigham's Hospital, the office manager showed me the types of documents the hospital routinely copied. One of the items was a sheet with several small pictures of some kind of scan.

"What are these?" I asked.

"Oh, those are copies of a patient's heart vectors," she replied.

I had no idea what a heart vector was but knew a good copy from a bad one.

"You can hardly see most of the information on this sheet."

"That's been a problem," she acknowledged. "We usually just use the original for evaluation and the copy for records."

"If you had a near-perfect copy of the original scan, would it be of any benefit?"

"Oh, god, yes! We hear complaints from the doctors all the time about these reproductions being such poor copies of the scans."

This was the opening I was looking for. Without hesitation, I handed her my brochure and started reviewing a few samples of the quality photos our equipment could reproduce before she became distracted by more pressing responsibilities. However, she was very receptive to my proposition and agreed to have a machine placed at the hospital for evaluation, providing there wasn't a cost associated with the trial.

WOW! Not only was it the largest and most expensive copier we handled, it was also the easiest for me because it was too big to fit into a car and had to be delivered and set up by service personnel. The hospital loved it and entered into a lease before the trial period was over. The machine needed expensive coated paper and toner to operate and they ran it nonstop. That lease and residual supply business from this transaction were among the largest in our company's history.

Shortly after this sale, I was given a larger section of downtown Boston as part of my expanded territory. I was able to use the reference of a major hospital account as a calling card on some of the prestigious law firms, insurance companies, and banks in the downtown market.

For the rest of my tenure with this employer, my sales kept me at first or second position in the company every month. However, I still longed for the opportunity to find a way to survive doing something in music, a passion still firmly implanted in my DNA.

TALENT AGENCY

ONE NIGHT, WHILE ORDERING take-out at a local Chinese restaurant, I noticed a fellow musician and friend setting up band equipment in the lounge.

"Hey man, how have you been? Your band is still together?" I asked, a little surprised.

"We have a new lead singer. Other than that, it's the same guys."

"What brings you up here?"

"Our agent booked us in this room for the next three weeks. It's our third time back. The pay's good, and the owner will let us eat for free." He laughed.

"Really?" I asked, sounding even more surprised. "You use an agent for this gig?"

"Northeast Entertainment, they book us everywhere. We're never out of work."

That chance encounter got me thinking. We used an

agent for our band when we were performing out of our area. It didn't appear to be a complicated function, and I had significant knowledge of the music business. How difficult could it be starting a new talent agency? I didn't wait another day. I dove in with both feet.

After various iterations, the company became known as Musicorp International, a talent agency that placed live entertainment in hotels and nightclubs throughout New England. At its peak, the agency controlled more than 30 locations weekly, with an artist roster exceeding 100 groups of various sizes and music styles. My goal was to have a nationally recognized recording act or two that would put the company into the upper end of the music business, with the requisite fame and fortune that would follow.

That didn't happen. What did happen was six to seven nights a week of traveling to the various venues, babysitting musicians, and assuring the owners and managers that they had the best entertainment their budgets could afford. It wasn't long before I realized that I was in the liquor business, not the music business. It didn't matter how talented the performers were; what determined the success of the engagement was how much money flowed into the registers. Days were spent making phone calls. Most of the time, we had all four lines tied up for hours playing checkers with the acts and owners trying to accommodate egos, schedules, money, equipment, and vehicles. At any moment, a band or an owner could cancel or a van packed with equipment get into an accident on the way to a sold-out show. Time off for vacations was not possible because of the demands of the business. It was an ongoing house of cards, requiring meticulous manipulation of all my physical, emotional, mental, and spiritual assets.

I smoked three packs of cigarettes a day and drank too much at night just trying to get to the next day without a major meltdown. My profession did look appealing from a distance. When I visited a venue, the bartenders and waitresses, manager, owner, and band members would vie for the opportunity to rub elbows with "the Agent." The recognition was usually short-lived, but it helped relieve the unrelenting grind to sit with clients and see a room full of their customers thoroughly appreciating my efforts.

Business Center

The agency was very successful, with income well above national averages, but it was a 12-hour-a-day, seven-day-a-week commitment, and I was always looking for a better opportunity to create income. My accountant approached me one day to ask if I would be interested in buying an office building with him. He said, "Many of my clients are investing in real estate and making very good returns." We were both located in the same small office building that was always 100% leased. "If we find a suitable office property, we will be the anchor tenants and lease the balance out to other businesses," he explained. His plan seemed like a good plan to me, so I started paying attention to For Sale signs on commercial properties in the area.

Within a few months of our discussion, a developer obtained the approvals to construct office condominiums on the same boulevard as our office. After meeting with the developer, my accountant and I decided to submit a purchase contract for the only free-standing building in phase one of the complex. My accountant asked if I would front the initial down payment because the bulk of his income was derived during tax season, and we were some months before that period. I was focused on the design concepts, and my accountant assumed responsibility for the financing processes. Finally, the big day arrived when the interior construction was to begin. I went to my partner's office so we could walk to the site together and observe the first row of partitions being set. This was going to be a really great day. It's an exciting process to see your ideas become a reality.

"Tom, I can't go with you today. One of my biggest clients had me send his tax files to a competitor." Continuing to pencil numbers in the green ledger book in front of him, he continued, "Not only that, but one of my other clients filed bankruptcy, and I doubt I'll ever get paid what he owes me."

"I'm sorry to hear that. I'll head over and let you know what they're doing when I get back."

Finally, dropping the pencil down onto the ledger, he looked to my right and then to my left. I knew that something was up; he couldn't make eye contact with me.

"Tom, I'm not going ahead with this project. I can't risk a single penny on a speculative project like this one. The market's a little soft right now, and very few investors are taking any risks. Besides, my business is too shaky. I'm really sorry, but you'll have to cancel the contract. I'm not going ahead with anything."

I couldn't believe what I was hearing. My thoughts became as scattered as a pile of fall leaves caught in a micro-burst. I had used most of my money for the down payment, and by now, it was non-refundable. What was I going to tell the contractor who had been so accommodating during all the drafting revisions? What about my reputation? What am I going to tell my wife, Carol? What do I do now?

One thing was perfectly clear. I wanted to go ahead with this project somehow. Since it had been my partner's job to secure financing, that was now going to be my first hurdle. Other than financing my house, I had no idea of how to initiate a loan on a commercial property. I made several calls the next morning to local banks asking to speak to a loan officer in the commercial lending department. The phone interviews went very well for the most part until the question of my experience and current occupation became center stage. Apparently, none of these lenders were knowledgeable about the talent-agency business. As intrigued as they were about the fact that I was somewhat successful at what I was doing, none had an interest in scheduling an in-person interview. One question they routinely asked referenced a business plan for the property. The loose idea of renting space to other users didn't seem to elicit much confidence.

A few nights later, after several hours of meditation about

my circumstances, a brainstorm started unfolding. I wrote down every idea that flowed into my mind. Within a few hours, a concept emerged that felt really right. In fact, it was so engaging that my thoughts weren't interrupted until daylight started to compete with my table lamp. I've always believed that ideas are in space, and at any time, any one of us can connect to these ideas that are specific to our current needs through simple meditation.

The talent agency needed one office, a reception area, and a conference room, which would accommodate less than 20% of the proposed building. This became the basis for the new concept. Why not share what every small office user needed but couldn't afford individually? At my current office, neighbors would routinely use my copier and fax. Sometimes the hairdresser next door needed a letter typed or borrowed stamps. Sometimes we were asked to sign for parcel deliveries when other tenants were out. I called the concept the Turn-Key Business Center, a shared-use office facility. Our clients would be provided a completely furnished private office and use of the reception area and conference room. Phones would be answered by a professional administrator, who also provided typing, copying, and faxing services and signatures for deliveries and would greet visitors to the facility. Although these arrangements are commonplace today, it was a radically new concept at that time. I had no idea if anyone else had ever thought of it—it was just an idea from space.

Armed with renewed enthusiasm, I went back to the contractor to adapt the floorplans one last time to the new innovation. With the conceptual drawings and a business plan to accompany them, I was able to find a lender willing to back the venture. My wife Carol and her assistant became the managers of the center, and I continued the talent agency business. Less than a year later, we had a waiting list of clients hoping to locate their business to our facility. Within three years, we received the proverbial offer that is "too good to refuse" for the business and real estate. That sale provided enough revenue to pay off our home mortgage and all other debts while leaving plenty of money for future opportunities. Life was very, very good!

TV

Encouraged by the success of the talent agency and business center, I felt I could accomplish anything. The fears that had haunted me back in the project days were long gone. I was ready for another challenge and started developing new ideas when a friend and business associate invited me to his recording studio in Boston to discuss his situation. He was financially strapped trying to pay rent in Boston and support his expensive payroll. His primary business was producing music jingles for radio and television advertisers. I wanted desperately to be involved in that type of business because our agency already represented some of the best musicians and writers in the greater Boston market. It would be a natural add-on and profit center for our company.

"You always have good ideas. Can you help me?" he pleaded, after giving me a tour of his recording studio. He described what the fate of his business would be unless he could identify a dramatic increase in revenue.

Somewhat surprised by his faith in my skills, I shared an idea with him in the early stages of development. Normally this would not be prudent, but considering his state of mind, I felt providing some hope was in order.

"I have an idea that could possibly help both of us find an exciting new career path. I call it 10 Magazine. It's a radio show about superlatives. For example, who are the 10 wealthiest people in the country and how did they make their money? Who are the 10 most powerful men and women, what are the 10 biggest hit records of all time, the 10 most haunted places, the 10 bestselling or most expensive cars, the 10 most expensive homes, the 10 best vacation destinations, the 10 highest-grossing movies of all time, the 10 most mysterious places on earth? You get the idea. The possibilities with 10 Magazine are unlimited." I explained that the broadcasts would be both entertaining and informative.

Prior to the internet, this information was very difficult and too time-consuming for the average person to find on their own. Our staff would include researchers acquiring this information from several resources.

Continuing the discussion, I speculated, "We could record the broadcasts here at your studio and syndicate them to radio stations across the country. With the equipment you already have, we could insert the sponsor's ad into the programs as an added benefit for the stations, saving them time and money."

My associate seemed to be interested but stopped the conversation rather abruptly. I wasn't sure if he thought I was crazy or he was so overwhelmed by his current problems that he couldn't sit still any longer. Either way, we parted company that day.

Several days later he invited me to his sister's house for a pool party. After the usual introductions and glass of wine, he said, "Tom, I've spoken to my attorney, and he tells me that you cannot copyright a general concept like 10 Magazine. I want you to be the first to know that my brothers and I intend to develop 10 Magazine into a television show with my brother as the host." Everything else he said that day is a blur. I was devastated to think a friend would compromise our relationship and plagiarize my concept so readily.

After reflecting on the situation for a few days, I realized his actions were motivated by preservation. He was trying to save his business and his image with his peers and family. I decided to call him to discuss a partnership of some kind. He was receptive to the idea, and the production company was formed with him, his three brothers, me, and an investor. We produced several shows that had great reviews and regional airplay, but never made any serious money due to the massive overhead of the staff and six partners. This was a setback; however, the income from the talent agency still provided a stable financial foundation to continue trying new ideas. I would have to leave my ambitions for TV and the jingle business for some time in the future.

YOUNG ADULT FACILITY

WITHIN MONTHS OF STOPPING production on the TV concepts, another friend and entertainment client wanted to start
a business. He and I would go to lunch and share ideas about
possible ventures. On one such occasion, we were trading war
stories about our life as band members on the road when I
recalled an engagement our manager had booked while we
were living in Chicago. It was a Dick Clark, Teen Scene Club.
In an instant, it was lightning strikes again. Ideas started
flowing nonstop for hours about how it could be structured.
The age group and personality profile we wanted to attract,
the type of entertainment, dress code, advertising, design
of the facility, communities in which we would operate, security, and finally a name, Traxx America—an upscale, no
alcohol, entertainment and dance facility for young adults
and college students over age 17. That meeting became the

starting point of our new endeavor. I was certain this would become the final destination for the rest of my working years.

Within a year, after overcoming all the usual challenges associated with this type of undertaking, we opened our first location. The VIP preview included Governor Mike Dukakis, journalist George Stephanopoulos, the town mayor, and virtually everyone who was anyone in town, all toasting to the success of this start-up venture with a glass of alcohol-free wine or beer. Almost immediately, Traxx was a spectacular hit—off the charts as the expression goes. Every weekend night, we could expect 500 customers inside the building and 200 waiting outside for the opportunity to be a part of the scene. New Kids on the Block appeared at Traxx to polish their routine before heading out on their first concert tour. Celebrity comedians graced our stage during our off-night comedy shows, and the local media, including Boston radio, promoted our success. We were the talk of the town. High school principals and community leaders were thanking us for providing such an incredible environment for the young adults of their city. Traxx America was the first facility of this type sanctioned by the SADD (Students Against Destructive Decisions) program. It just doesn't get any better.

I was 40 years old, with enough income and assets that retirement at 50 was more than just a possibility. Although that was not my intention, it was fun to think it was achievable.

During the first year of operation, only a few minor

incidents needed attention: the usual girlfriend-boyfriend disputes and the occasional territorial conflicts common to that age group. We even impressed ourselves at how well run the operations were. With the exception of security, local college kids were our primary employees. They loved the action and did a remarkable job. There was a waiting list of students hoping to be called for the next available position. The entertainment schedule also appealed to a diverse group, which kept the off nights busy. The music programming proved to be one of the most effective tools in attracting the clientele we wanted. Our security systems had matured, and the dress code also made a night out at Traxx America special, regardless of how many times you participated in this fashionable social environment.

With everything in place, it was time to move to the next level. After talking with several business and financial consultants, it was decided that we would franchise the concept so we could open multiple locations simultaneously and capitalize on the success of the initial Traxx America. In order to finance the venture, we would need to sell the existing facility and become the corporate people instead of the operators of the business. It didn't take long to find willing franchisees ready to invest more than seven figures for the opportunity to share in our success. We had a purchase and sales agreement for the existing facility within a few weeks. The town where our next location was to be developed sent a group of officials to investigate the concept before voting to permit the facility. They were very impressed and excited about a facility of this type in their community. We had a tiger by the tail!

In the middle of all our euphoria, we received a registered letter from the district court informing us we were named as defendants in a lawsuit filed on behalf of an injured patron. The incident in question occurred on Friday, February 13, almost a year earlier. One of our employees brought a date to the facility on her off night. They were allowed through security at the front door and at the cashier window because employees and their dates were not required to pay for admittance. It was a flaw in our security system. Later we learned that he had consumed a few cans of beer at his escort's apartment, located across the street from our facility, before entering that night. Even if he had entered through the normal security system in place, his condition might not have been detected. An hour or so after his arrival, he took a swing at another patron whom he believed had made a disparaging remark to his girlfriend. In self-defense, the other person struck back, hitting the antagonist in the mouth and knocking out one of his teeth. Security personnel quickly quelled the altercation before it escalated any further. We immediately called for an ambulance, stopped the music, and turned up the lights. We located the missing tooth, placed it in a bottled-water container, and delivered it to the hospital as instructed by the attending EMT personnel. Although this person instigated the situation, we felt obligated to do what we could to assist him. We spoke to his parents and asked what we could do that could make a difference for them. We also offered to pay for any dental costs. It certainly appeared as though everyone involved recognized that this was an unfortunate incident but not uncommon or unexpected when a room full of young adults are congregating.

However, a year later, we were defendants in a sizable lawsuit. The timing couldn't have been worse. Our franchisee for the new location was right at the point of completing his affiliation agreement after receiving approvals from the town and his bank. Several others were in the cue, and the franchisee now in control of the original operation was pressing us to begin the coordinated advertising and entertainment schedule we had agreed to implement within a certain timeframe or face penalties. The more locations that are open, the lower the ad cost per unit, because the costs are shared. Having the ability to offer entertainers multiple locations to perform would place our venue on their preferred list. Both the advertising and entertainment programs needed an operating second location to take effect. Unfortunately, all expansion efforts were put on hold pending the outcome of the suit. Although the basis of the suit was weak, lenders would not fund loans with an unresolved court case because juries are not predictable in their awards.

Things quickly went from bad to worse. When we sold the original facility, we accepted a promissory note for a part of the sale price. Since we were unsuccessful in developing additional facilities within the expected timeframe, the operator decided we had technically violated our arrangement with him, and he no longer felt obligated to make loan payments or the franchise fees. This meant we would have to engage in another lawsuit with our franchisee to recover our money. He also decided at that time to make several changes in the way the concept was operated. A family member was put in charge of music selection, and he abandoned our very successful programming format. Within months, the operation was a shell of its original concept. No dress code, no age limits, no restricted music, lax security, and elimination of special events for college students. Traxx America no longer represented a special place for special nights. It had become a second-rate operation that could be located in an industrial warehouse instead of a high-end Las Vegas-style nightclub in the heart of the community.

Several months later, the lawsuit was settled, without prejudice, before the case went to trial. In other words, the plaintiff decided they couldn't win the suit but didn't want to end up with a large legal bill and other expenses either. On the advice of our attorney, we agreed to the settlement, but the damage was done. Traxx was finished for the foreseeable future. The suit had negated our expansion plans, and a short time later, the original facility was closed. What was once a thrilling adventure had become a heartbreaking turn of events.

ADVERTISING MUSIC PRODUCTION

BOTH MY PARTNER AND I HAD a music background and were familiar with the recording industry. The old desire to someday be a part of the burgeoning jingle and music production side of the advertising industry seemed like a logical direction for both of us. We still had enough money in our business account from the sale of the real estate and enough retained earnings from the operations at Traxx America to initiate a new plan. We purchased a couple of office condominiums and hired a prominent recording studio designer to implement a state-of-the-art, digital audio recording facility. Our technology was so current that the operating system the designer installed was still in its beta testing phase. Construction took twice as long and cost nearly twice as much as what we had initially budgeted.

When we were finally ready for our grand opening almost a year later, it was with mixed emotions. We had been here before and recognized that nothing is guaranteed. We believed we did everything right in our previous venture, and it ended badly. Still, the excitement of attracting the top movers and shakers in the advertising industry to our facility was energizing. Similar to our earlier business, this grand opening received rave reviews by all attendees and local press covering the event. Our decision to hire an acclaimed Boston engineer with strong ties to chart-topping recording artists, including Aerosmith and Debbie Gibson, also added credibility to our effort.

Once we were in the flow of the business, we started producing some of the best radio spots airing within our market, including some of the top Boston stations. Our clients and the reps at these radio stations consistently rated our work as outstanding and innovative in every category, including music production, copy, voice-over talent, and overall quality of production. We were logging more than 60 hours a week trying to build a clientele large enough to support our enormous overhead. However, after the first year of operation, it became apparent that we were not going to have the raging success we experienced with our previous venture. We were losing money every week. It cost two to three times as much to produce our commercials as our clients were willing to pay for them. The fees to writers, musicians, engineers, and our basic premium overhead were draining our assets at an astonishing rate. Not only were we losing money at work, but we also didn't draw a salary. It wasn't long before our business and personal finances were in a death spiral.

The entire advertising industry was going through a very difficult period; however, they were not alone. The commercial real estate market was also in a steep decline, affecting the values of property everywhere, but especially in the Northeast. Even Donald Trump had to find creative ways to keep his New York portfolio from foreclosure. Although we were making payments at the time, our bank informed us that we were in a technical default of the loan provisions because the underlying value of our office condominiums had fallen below the minimum requirement of equity on a commercial property. Simply put, we needed more money down to keep our loan in compliance. When we purchased the units, we put 50% down and paid cash for all the improvements, which exceeded the cost of the units. It seemed outrageous that we could be in this position. Cash was extremely tight and putting more capital into the real estate was nearly impossible. We needed every dollar to continue funding the business. This was the tipping point for my partner. He didn't want to invest any more money into a venture with such a dubious outcome, so we amicably dissolved the partnership. He remains one of my closest friends and advisors.

When my youngest daughter was less than one year old, Carol and I had started planning for her college by funding a savings account intended for that future need. We decided to close the account and also take the cash value of a sizable retirement annuity to satisfy the loan deficit and get on with the business—but what business? It was obvious to me that the traditional jingle industry was not going to be profitable quick enough for me to save the business from failure. New ideas were needed. It was difficult to ask Carol to participate in these failed efforts, but I couldn't see any other way forward.

One of the successful projects our efforts at the recording studio had completed was the placement of Robert Parker's Jazz Classics on Public Radio International. The show was aired nationwide for five seasons. What is interesting about public radio and TV is that they do not air traditional commercials for their sponsors. They use short, to-the-point statements that brand the sponsor, such as American Express ("Don't leave home without it."), General Electric ("We bring good things to Life."), the military ("Be all that you can be in the Army."), De Beers ("A Diamond is Forever."), Nike ("Just Do It!"). No additional copy is used, but the to-the-point tag lines clearly identify the sponsor and provide a summary of their message. It is very effective.

Using that simple idea, we developed a series of programs that would be interesting to the listeners and then inserted a brief but profound message about the sponsor at the beginning and end of the spot. Research showed that listeners could more easily remember a short statement than a full one-minute commercial. We used a custom-music signature to alert listeners that one of the "special commercials" was about to air. The content of the program would be comedy, entertainment news, biographies, or other interesting subject matter not usually found in the regular programming of the radio station. The biggest issue at the time was delivery of the programming, since it changed every day. We would need more writers, administrative assistants, studio personnel, and salespeople to make it all work. Early test marketing with the programming directors at several key stations was very positive. It appeared that a turning point was at hand. We'd found a path to success.

The next big issue was funding the new project. It had been close to four years without a paycheck, and resources were diminishing. My savings account was depleted, so I took loans on the remaining insurance policies we owned. Most had been purchased in my early 20s and had accumulated high values. We also refinanced our house to gain access to the accumulated equity. In less than six months, however, all that cash was gone. In frantic desperation to continue the project, I elected to form a partnership with three investors.

We were all confident the programs would be successful if development of the concept continued.

Within two weeks of receiving the investment funds, our friendly bank stepped back into the picture and informed us that they no longer intended to underwrite loans on office condos. Our existing loan term was expiring, and it would not be extended. We had 45 days to pay up or face possible foreclosure. The office condos housed our recording studio and staff offices. Just when it appeared everything was going to work out perfectly, a whole new conflict emerged for us to manage.

I was already struggling to make the mortgage payments at home, obviating the possibility of finding a bank to rescue the commercial property. The investors were not willing to add funds to what now appeared to be a losing proposition, especially if the real estate was removed from the equation. At this point, the only possible solution was to find another private party to become the bank and sell our home to lower our monthly obligations. One of my neighbors who was aware of the situation negotiated a buy-out with the lender and took a high-interest, first mortgage on the property. Not a perfect solution, but at least we had a place to continue our work, as long as we could make our mortgage payments.

Sales continued to be very slow for the next several months because we couldn't afford the manpower need- ed to mass market the programs, a necessity to becoming profitable. Also, home sales were almost nonexistent in our market, and the capital needed to fund my personal expenses was now primarily coming from credit cards. I was at my limit financially. Few sales, no personal income for years, and falling prices on residential and commercial real estate began to overwhelm me. The impact on my marriage was also mounting. Carol had always been my number-one fan. Now she was spending most of her day fielding calls from credit card companies who were demanding payments. She wanted me out of the recording business and out looking for a job that had a paycheck attached to it. She didn't care if it was flipping burgers at McDonald's as long as it paid for groceries. She had no control over the circumstances that brought us to this point. Her position was clearly understandable. It was another predicament adding to the expanding stack of adversities that needed to be addressed.

REVERSAL OF FORTUNE

EVENTUALLY, THE HOUSE SOLD AT a deep reduction from what we paid, eroding all the remaining equity in the property. We located a low-cost rental in the community that would allow our daughter to stay in the same school system. It was the only small victory during this time.

It's amazing how some people treat you—as if your financial condition were contagious. One of our contractor clients from the ad agency was hired to remove a small in-ground oil tank used to heat our pool. It had to be done prior to closing on our house. That night, when I returned home from work, he was waiting in the driveway to collect his money. I told him I was tired and would drop a check off in the morning because the only account with money was back at the office. "I'm here now, I'll wait," he said.

Our ad agency had produced his company's commercials and purchased the radio time to broadcast the message. His company was always 60 to 90 days behind in payments. We had to pay the radio station invoices within 30 days to avoid late fees and the possibility of being shut off from booking additional airtime slots for our other clients. I never went to his company to wait for a check, even though our exposure was substantially higher than his. I knew his company would pay as soon as they could, but now I was on the other end of the invoice. It was very uncomfortable not being trusted with even a small amount of money by someone I considered a friend. He was not the only one. The angel neighbor started micromanaging payments of condo fees and taxes on the studio property. Even my former partner remarked while helping us move to the rental property, "I didn't know Bedford had slums." I know it was just a joke. Bedford doesn't have any slums, but the point brought home my uncomfortable new reality.

Every day seemed worse than the day before, with no relief in sight. I continually felt as if I were plowing the ocean. When one problem was addressed, another two were waiting to take its place. How could this have happened to me? How could I lose everything? All that money earned from years trudging through the streets of Boston selling copy equipment, the thousands of nights out managing the chaos of the entertainment business, the income from the business center, the income from the young adult club, plus all the equity and improvements that went into our home, all gone. Everything Carol had contributed was also sucked into the vacuum.

I was totally spent. It felt as though every waking moment was a permanent punch in the gut. I just wanted to lie down and never wake up, but even sleep wouldn't let me escape the nightmare. Several times each night I would awaken in sheer panic, wondering if we would become a homeless family, or need to live off the generosity of others. There was no solution in sight. The hopelessness of our situation was painfully obvious to me every minute of every day. How did I go from being wealthy at 40 to renting a starter home at 48, with no prospects of recovery? I believed that someday I would have a great story to tell. Now the only story I had to convey was one nobody wanted to listen to. Trying to find some comfort by escaping into memories of the good old days was also a wasted effort. Nothing was working to relieve the paralysis.

Most of the next year was a continuation of the same aimless existence. Managing the credit card companies and their relentless calling, trying to pay rent, and putting groceries on the table now posed a challenge for us as difficult as the one my mother faced when we were kids living in the project. Carol and I did everything possible to minimize the effect our situation would have on our youngest daughter, but even that was becoming more difficult to camouflage. Little by little, we were all sinking into a depressed state. Most of my time was spent making excuses to everyone, including myself, for our current state of affairs. It was embarrassing to run into friends and acquaintances, wondering what they were thinking. What little income I could take from the studio and Carol's salary barely provided the essentials. Forget about any extras.

During this time, even the IRS demanded thousands of dollars in back taxes and interest. A few years earlier, I would have simply written the check without hesitation or concern. Now the added payments to the IRS made an impossible situation even more hopeless. There was always something every day to add to the desperation. I started anticipating all the bad things that could still happen to my family and expected those dreaded events to occur at any moment. It is amazing how fast a reversal of fortune can collapse even the most determined spirit and hide everything but the pain around you. Simply breathing becomes a chore. I didn't think it was possible to be so beat up and still be alive.

THE AWAKENING

ONE NIGHT I WENT FOR A LONG WALK back to the old neighborhood. Walking past our former home, I hid behind the bushes near the driveway entrance and started reflecting on what put me on the outside looking in. Hours went by, reminiscing about the move-in, the renovations, the parties, the holidays, the fun we had in the backyard sandbox and pool, the first cars for our teenagers, who were now out on their own—so many memories. Was this it for me? Would there ever be something good in my future to remember? As the night progressed, I felt a transition starting to take place within. My mood migrated from pensive, to angry, to fed up with my current existence. I was rapidly approaching 50 years old, and the thought of starting over...over 50 seemed impossible. Yet I knew I could no longer live the way I had been. I wanted my life back. The one where I controlled my future, not the credit card companies, not the IRS, not the bank or the circumstances of that day, just me!

Several years earlier, while I was working at the copier company, I met the owner of a local insurance agency. He wasn't interested in purchasing our copying equipment, but that day he provided me with something far more valuable than a sale.

"We both agree your company's products do not fit my needs," my prospect began, "but I want you to know I am very impressed with you. You took the time to make sure you had all the facts about our requirements and are honest about the limitations of your equipment. You didn't try to sell me. You helped me make the right decision for my firm, and I appreciate it. I want you to have a copy of this book we hand out to our new agents. Hopefully, the ideas in here will help you. I know it's been a big help to me and many others here."

It was a very small book, less than 50 pages, but it contained one very interesting premise: that your thoughts will determine your future. It was a revolutionary concept for me at that time. I never considered my circumstances had much to do with me. I assumed that circumstances were more a matter of fate than self-programming. A short time later, I came across a copy of Napoleon Hill's book, Think and Grow Rich, required reading for anyone looking to attain higher levels of achievement. I was hooked. I became a self-improvement junky. I bought books, tapes, and magazine subscriptions and attended seminars by motivational authors and speakers. I started writing down goals. I quit smoking, began an exercise program, and developed a positive mental attitude from the wealth of information available in the market. Most of my successful ventures had been a direct result of the awareness that controlling your thoughts and establishing goals will, by default, determine a significant part of your future.

So, what had happened to me? I'd never started having negative thoughts. I'd written down my goals. I knew where I wanted to go. Was all the motivational hype just that? Hype?! Is it real, or is it for only a few select individuals who would have been successful anyway, without the knowledge crafted by the authors and philosophers of the self-improvement genre? Did I miss something? Why am I the one who's looking from behind the bushes?

"I cannot live another minute like this," I said, my voice so loud I was afraid everyone in the old neighborhood had heard me. Brian Tracy wrote in one of his books, "No one is coming to the rescue. If it is to be, you have to do it." That quote echoed in my mind over and over that night. No one is coming to the rescue; I have to do it. No one is coming to the rescue; I have to do it. No one is coming to the rescue; I have to do it!

That night, on my walk back to the rental property, I

made the decision to find a way to start over. I also decided to reread all the books, listen to the tapes and CDs, and put to the test all the promises of success in those writings. This was the first time in more than three years that I felt like myself. As the saying goes, "I've had enough, and I'm not going to take it anymore!" Tony Robbins was right when he observed that we all have a giant within because there was an angry giant beginning to awaken in me.

As soon as I returned home, I started committing to paper a prolific list of the goals I intended to begin implementing. The night passed, and soon the sun was rising, along with the certainty that I had lived to face another day. Surprisingly, I wasn't tired—quite the opposite. I used the sunlight breaching the windows to cast shadow puppets on the wall, reinforcing the fact that I was still alive and could still cast shadows. Today would be a possibility day, not my usual what else can go wrong day. My anger over all the past losses was migrating quickly into a resolve and determination to regain control of my circumstances and start over.

The big question I kept asking myself was, "How do I start over at my age with no college degree, so much debt, and no money?" Starting over over 50 carries challenges that are unique to that age. Real and imagined obstacles dominate every second of your thought process. Seeing a way out is further diminished because the perceived assets of youth are considered waning after 50. However, starting over was my new mission, and I was determined to start that day, regardless of the outcome. I could still cast shadows, and I wanted to cast more than hand puppets. The lingering question was, "WHAT DO I DO"?

STARTING OVER . . .
OVER 50

I STARTED BY WRITING A LIST of every job I had done in the past and included activities that I was proficient in or enjoyed doing. It was amazing how many possibilities became apparent from that list. However, without any money or highly specialized training, the only choice for me would be an occupation that offered a personal service. Earlier experience in sales and working with nightclub, hotel, and restaurant operators pointed to a possible career as a real estate person representing hospitality operators who wanted to sell their business and real estate. Instead of representing their talent, I could represent their properties.

Years earlier, the developer of the office park where the business center was located said that he could not develop the next phase of the project until he sold out phase one and had at least four pre-sales in phase two.

"What seems to be the problem, Bob?" I asked him. "These units should all be sold considering the great location and reasonable prices."

"Several people are interested, but no one's signing on the bottom line," he explained. "We're using a top broker and advertising in all the pertinent media. It's just a tough market right now."

The building where the talent agency had previously operated was in need of updating, and the rents were fairly high. Most of the tenants there were ideal prospects for buying their own office condominiums on the same boulevard, just as I had done.

"I know several people who might be interested, Bob. Do you want me to talk to them?"

"If you had a real estate license, Tom, you could co-broker the sales with my broker."

One of our clients at the business center was a residential real estate broker. I asked her if I could apply for a real estate license and place it with her firm so I could legally solicit potential buyers for the unbuilt units in our development. She agreed, and after I was licensed, we began marketing the units to my business associates and other renters nearby. We were directly responsible for the sale of 12 units over the next few months, more than enough for the developer to secure his financial arrangements and complete the project.

This brief commercial real estate experience, combined with my knowledge of the nightclub, restaurant, and hospitality industry, made my decision to start a commercial real estate firm seem like the best possibility for producing income with such limited resources.

Similar to all new start-ups, the first year was extremely difficult. It was obvious that success in the commercial real estate business was going to take considerable effort, planning, and persistence. Without the opportunity to work in an established firm, the learning curve was intense. I invested every spare minute in reading pertinent materials and talking with notable brokers in hopes of learning the secrets of their success.

The second year was much better, and by the time the business entered its fourth year, it was obvious that this was the right career choice. The company produced enough revenue to pay off all of the credit card debt, provide the opportunity to build a new home, and place a bank loan on the commercial real estate condominiums, releasing my angel neighbor from any further obligations. Over the next 10 years, the company produced enough income to pay off our home mortgage and the commercial mortgages. The investors who were part of the failed limited partnership received their investment back in full, and my youngest daughter graduated cum laude from Northeastern University in Boston without needing any student loans. In addition, the combined value of our assets was substantially above the level they were before the meltdown. We were back, 100%.

No one was more amazed at the success of our company than I was. However, reporting that my situation changed from rags to riches overnight would be a colossal misrepresentation of the process. It was hard. It was very hard, but I learned something surprising. With all my knowledge of the tools to success, it's what I didn't know that tripped me up at the height of my career and put me on the road to failure. These insights will be discussed later. Intense reflection also revealed that the road back to success is possible at any age if you utilize the Essential Common Denominators of Success. No one can possess lasting achievement without strict adherence to these principles, with or without a person's awareness that these principles are having a substantial effect on them. Great men of every generation have reaffirmed the existence of these principles and the power afforded to those who master them. They have not changed in thousands of years and will not as long as we exist. They are part of the natural laws governing the universe and all individuals that reside within it. Awareness of the Essential Common Denominators of Success will afford you the opportunity to choose between an accidental life and a designed one.

THE ESSENTIAL COMMON DENOMINATORS OF SUCCESS

THE ESSENTIAL COMMON DENOMINATORS of Success are listed here in an abbreviated form. There are many common denominators that all people share and many that only some share. The happiest and most successful people share all of them and benefit from the impact these traits have had on their lives. Financial and career success without happiness is not success. It is happiness and joy that elevates the human condition to its highest level. Although not mandatory, most people do not experience these higher states of being without some degree of success in their careers and the requisite financial freedom that provides the balance they need in their lives.

1. Unique: We are all a one-off specimen. No two people are exactly alike. If we do not accomplish our mission here, no one else can do it for us. Happy and successful people believe they are here for a reason. Most religions promote this enlightened view of our existence.

2. Responsibility: All happy and successful people accept responsibility for their own actions. They do not blame others for their failures because they realize that failure is an important component of ultimate success. They do not look to others to relieve them of their responsibilities or embrace excuses. They address unpleasant circumstances head-on.

3. Time: Time is precious but also relentless. Proper use of the time allotted to us is critical to fulfill our lives' purpose. Happy and successful people recognize that time is the most valuable resource and that it can only be used in the present, and they do not waste it. They use their time for the joy of living, personal improvement, accomplishment, and the benefit of sharing quality time with others. They recognize that happiness and joy can be experienced only in the here and now and not at some future point.

4. Choice: This is the driver of the bus. Happy and successful people choose to be that way. They make

good choices in everyday decisions that lead them to the outcomes they desire and expect.

5. Goals: All happy and successful people have a good idea of where they want to be at any given time in their lives. Most have established goals and a very clear direction for their future. They do not rely on wishing and hoping. They are doers.

6. Thoughts: Thoughts are things! Thoughts are things! Thoughts are things! You become what you think about most, a self-fulfilling prophecy, as Earl Nightingale positions it. Happy and successful people control their thoughts, recognizing that these cliché definitions about the power of thought are accurate.

7. Focus: It is virtually impossible to accomplish anything of value without focus. Scattering your attention in a hundred different directions diffuses your energy and almost always ends badly. Focus has magical powers for getting things done. Without focus, it is easy to confuse activity with productivity.

8. Change: We live in a dynamic universe. Change is inevitable. Happy and successful people recognize this and accept it rather than fear change. They adapt to their current conditions and direct their efforts and resources to the new realities of the day. It is

part of the natural rhythm of life that happy and successful people embrace.

9. Faith and Belief: Happy and successful people believe in themselves and have faith that their current and future endeavors will be successful and fulfilling. Goodness and confidence are byproducts of a strong faith in a higher authority. Faith and fear cannot occupy the same space at the same time. Without fear, much can be accomplished.

10. Sow and Reap: What goes around comes around, also known as karma and reciprocity. Happy and successful people plant seeds of love, cooperation, goodness, and honesty. They share resources and have genuine empathy for their fellow travelers. They never expect something for nothing, because they understand that without planting adequate seeds, there will not be an adequate harvest.

WE ARE ALL UNIQUE

"Everyone has his own specific vocation or mission in life to carry out a concrete assignment which demands fulfillment. Therein he cannot be replaced, nor can his life be repeated. Thus, everyone's task is as unique as his specific opportunity to implement it." —Viktor Frankl

HOMELESS OR RESIDING IN THE WHITE HOUSE, we are all a single copy. No one before us or after us will ever be exactly alike. It is a recurring theme of esteemed thinkers who have recognized the uniqueness of every individual. Cave drawings, Old Testament passages, and observations made by modern-day scientists and philosophers herald this distinctiveness, which is now supported by the mapping of the human genome and DNA research. Simply put, you are irreplaceable.

Without your contributions, the entire universe is

diminished. Sounds ominous, but it's true. None of us is here by accident. There are no mistakes in nature, only our misunderstanding of the process. We have a responsibility to be the person we were intended to be, and only the individual can make the determination of what that person will be. Apathy is a dereliction of our obligation to ourselves and humanity. We need to be proactive in employing our talents or risk losing them. All of us have an innate desire to achieve something worthwhile. It is part of the DNA of humanity, but it does take action on our part.

A parable in the Bible relates a story about the master of a large estate leaving for an extended period of time and entrusting his servants with valuable coins. This story is the perfect illustration of "Use it or lose it." When the master returns, he asks for an accounting. The first servant received five coins and doubled that amount through proper investing. The second was given two coins, and like the first servant, also doubled his money. The third servant, who was entrusted with only one coin, hid the coin and only returned the one he was given. The master praised the first two servants and elevated them to higher positions of authority and responsibility, and with greater compensation, whereas the third servant was removed from his position and banished from the estate. His coin was divided between the other two servants. The takeaway? The coins represent the native talents all of us are endowed with at birth. To those who use their talents, more will be given, and to those who do not, what little they have will be taken away.

Age is an advantage, not an excuse. Being over 50 should be celebrated. It is a milestone of significant importance. Although some physical talents may be diminished, they are being replaced with equal or greater experience talents that can only be acquired through time. Even a person with very limited resources can accomplish something that elevates their condition. Lack of ambition or desire to accomplish one's mission is usually at fault for a lingering failure. None of us are without the ability to achieve. Some of the humblest of our predecessors have left the deepest footprints in the sands of time.

Identify and employ your unique talents before time eradicates their usefulness. We are all gifted with exclusive capabilities because no other person could have experienced the exact sequence of events from childhood through adulthood that we have. Dr. Edmond Locard, the pioneer of forensic science, recognized that "every contact leaves a trace." It is the same in our lives. Every experience, every relationship, our education, our associates, our musical preferences, our physical and mental capabilities, our attitudes and opinions all contribute to our uniqueness. Every day we live leaves a trace on our whole being. Accept and appreciate your uniqueness and utilize your valuable resources to start your recovery. As Erma Bombeck said, "When I stand before God at the end of my life, I would hope that I would not have a single bit of talent left and could say, I used everything you gave me."

We Are a Composite of Our Collective Knowledge

"We are each gifted in a unique and important way. It is our privilege and our adventure to discover our own special light." —Mary Dunbar

WHEN ROBERT KEARNS DEVELOPED the intermittent wiper system, car manufacturers did not want to compensate him for the invention because they claimed that no new components were used in his design. Kearns instituted a lawsuit demanding compensation and recognition for his invention. The manufacturer's defense claimed that the end product was just a combination of existing transistors and resistors configured in a different way. Kearns, in his rebuttal, began reciting very common words and asked the jury if they had ever heard them before. They all acknowledged that they are common words. He then asked the jury if they thought these words could be found in a dictionary. Again, they confirmed that all the words he presented would be found in any dictionary.

He then recited the common words in this order:

It was the best of times, it was the worst of times, it was the age of wisdom, it was the age of foolishness, it was the epoch of belief, it was the epoch of incredulity, it was the season of Light, it was the season of Darkness, it was the spring of hope, it was the winter of despair...

Kearns had read the opening of Charles Dickens's *A Tale of Two Cities*. It consisted of common words placed in an imaginative and original order to compose one of the most profound opening paragraphs in English literature. By the time his lawsuits were over, Kearns had received the recognition he wanted and more than $30 million in compensation for his unique placement of existing transistors and resistors.

Starting over at any age requires focus and persistence for success. However, starting over when you're over 50 has some very distinct advantages. Just as humanity today has the benefit of the collective knowledge of all the previous generations, you also have the accumulated knowledge of your own experiences to guide you into your future. No one has had the exact experience that is singularly yours and that collective knowledge, integrated with your individual uniqueness, is very valuable, just like the resistors and transistors of Kearns' invention or the common words placed together by Charles Dickens. The path to success in my personal rejuvenation was the aggregate knowledge I possessed from a myriad of previous activities. The same is true of every individual over 50. Your accumulated knowledge and skills required time to develop. If you needed open-heart surgery to save your life, would you choose the doctor just out of medical school or the 50-year-old doctor who has performed the exact procedure successfully a multitude of times? Most would opt for the experienced doctor.

ONE PERSON CAN
CHANGE THE WORLD

"Never forget that you are one of a kind. Never forget that if there weren't any need for you in all your uniqueness to be on this earth, you wouldn't be here in the first place. And never forget, no matter how overwhelming life's challenges and problems seem to be, that one person can make a difference in the world. In fact, it is always because of one person that all the changes in the world come about. So be that person."
—Buckminster Fuller

WHEN I WAS IN MY EARLY 20S, a couple whom my wife and I met for dinner from time to time suggested that we try General Glover's restaurant, located in Saugus, Massachusetts, a small community just north of Boston. The back of the menu had a simple story about the man for whom the restaurant was named.

In 1777, both the colonists and the British command believed that the American Revolution was nearing an unsuccessful end. The Continental Army under the command of George Washington was reduced to a small embattled force of untrained and starving troops barely surviving in Valley Forge, Pennsylvania, during the winter of that year. Washington was desperate for some kind of victory to keep his army from disbanding. Across the river from Valley Forge lay the Town of Trenton, New Jersey, currently occupied by Hessian soldiers, a highly trained mercenary army under the employ of the British. Washington decided to attack the fortified garrison the morning of December 26, the day after Christmas, hoping to have the element of surprise on his side. In order to do this, he needed to cross the Delaware River with more than 2,400 troops, horses, supplies, and artillery between dusk and dawn, using only a few boats commandeered from some of the residents living in the area. Adding to the logistical nightmare were the weather conditions. The river had large ice flows and just as the maneuvers were to get underway, a blinding snowstorm developed. Time was critical because Washington had to arrive at the outpost by daylight, before the Hessian soldiers recovered from the Christmas celebrations the night before.

Colonial John Glover from Marblehead, Massachusetts,

was an experienced fisherman and owner of several fishing vessels before the war. His unique knowledge was just what was needed that night. He and his fellow militiamen from Marblehead were accustomed to the severe conditions of coastal New England waters and had navigated through many of the enormous storms that develop in that area. They organized the crossing with such precision and speed that, even by today's standards, its success would be considered highly improbable. But complete it they did! Washington and his men surprised the unsuspecting army, claimed the much-needed victory, and returned to Valley Forge with more than 900 prisoners. Even more incredible is that not one of Washington's men was killed in the engagement. One of the two wounded soldiers was James Monroe, who later became the fifth president of the United States. Moreover, this victory encouraged a significant number of sympathetic colonists to enlist and prompted Congress to continue funding the Continental Army. Without it, the Revolutionary War would have been lost, and the history of the world would be different.

One man, bringing his collective and specialized knowledge to a receptive team of other individuals, had brought about a dramatic and profound outcome. Glover was later elevated to major general and is considered by many locals from Marblehead as the man who saved the Revolution. A volunteer who brought his unique skills to the battlefield at great personal cost, he is an example of how valuable every individual is to society, whether they are famous or little known.

EXPERIENCE IS NOT OVERRATED

"Knowledge by definition makes itself obsolete.
Skills last forever." —Peter Drucker

ON A SUNNY THURSDAY AFTERNOON, a routine US Airways flight from LaGuardia Airport in New York City departed for Seattle. At the most critical point of the ascent, the plane collided with a flock of Canada geese. The impact immediately shut down both jet engines. Without propulsion, and at a low altitude, the aircraft was in catastrophic failure. The air traffic controller recommended that the pilot attempt an emergency landing across the river in New Jersey at a small airport away from the urban sprawl that lay in its immediate flight path. The controller knew the situation was dire and wanted the inevitable crash to occur where emergency crews could respond immediately. With only a few seconds to assess the situation, the captain evaluated the options and decided to attempt a water landing in the Hudson River instead of at the small airport.

Most water landings end badly because the plane usually cartwheels or flips across the surface, breaks apart, and sinks quickly. The prognosis for the captain, crew, and passengers at that moment was bleak. The pilot, Chesley Sullenberger, or Sully as his colleagues call him, had extensive glider experience from his military service years earlier and had logged thousands of hours of flight time as a commercial pilot. He not only landed the powerless plane in the river, but he did it with such precision that the aircraft remained intact and floated long enough to evacuate every passenger and crew member safely. Amazingly, not a single person was lost that day.

If we were to add all the relatives, friends, and colleagues of the 155 passengers and crew, a catastrophe on that day would have affected thousands and possibly millions of people, when you calculate the collective loss of all the contributions those individuals would have made to their families and society. Everyone on that flight—and the rest of the world—witnessed the value of Captain Sullenberger's experience and knowledge in action.

Experience is still the greatest teacher, and we can all benefit from the collective knowledge of the generations that went before us. There is a reason why cave dwellers didn't have airplanes. Their collective knowledge at the time didn't support that possibility. Very successful men and woman throughout the ages have understood the value of specialized and collective knowledge. Those great people who have lived and died can no longer actively contribute to our collective knowledge, but you can. The accumulated experiences of your life are the building blocks you need to reframe your life the way you want it to be. This is your specialized knowledge, just as Sully's and General Glover's experiences were theirs. The Hindu religion refers to one's proper role in life as dharma. Everyone is unique and everyone has a purpose for being here, a dharma. It's not a mistake. You belong here, or you wouldn't be here.

RESPONSIBILITY

"The price of greatness is responsibility."
—Winston Churchill

BEFORE YOU CAN MAKE ANY SERIOUS progress on your future ambitions, there is one more difficult hurdle to overcome, and that is responsibility. It is impossible to start over without first accepting responsibility for your current condition, accepting responsibility for your thoughts, and accepting responsibility for a recovery. Don't blame the bank, your spouse, your kids, your business associates, the economy, the government, or the family pet. Even if someone or something else is truly the responsible party for your current situation, do not seek revenge. It will significantly diminish your focus. Bury the past. It is fixed and cannot be changed. It's hard enough navigating the comeback trail without a 100-pound sack of grudges on your back. As Gandhi recognized, *"The weak can never forgive. Forgiveness is an attribute of the strong.*" And Nelson Mandela once remarked, *"When a deep injury is done to us, we never heal until we forgive."* In other words, you may not want to hug some people, but you must forgive, forget, and move on. This is for your benefit, not theirs.

It's easy to be in denial about our circumstances, and we often fail to act responsibly by not accepting the reality of our situation. Barry D. retained a broker from our firm to list a $9 million investment property he had acquired on Martha's Vineyard. Normally, it would take an entire day to arrive on the Vineyard from New Hampshire because of the distance, traffic, and ferry schedules to the island. Instead, Barry flew us to the property in about 30 minutes using his private jet. Later that evening, an associate of Barry explained that he was seriously overinvested in residential building lots in an upscale community in the greater Boston area. The debt payments on his holdings were crippling his cash flow, and sales of high-end lots were almost nonexistent during the Great Recession. In addition to his personal residence, he owned a second vacation property on the Vineyard, another on a mountaintop at a ski resort in Vermont, and still another on the Maine coast. The expenses alone on those other properties were staggering. The same was true for his private jet. I asked Barry's associate the obvious question. "Why doesn't Barry sell all these properties and the private jet? All are cash drains and do not produce any income.

He can consolidate to his personal residence and sell all his non-essential assets until the market improves."

The explanation offered was that Barry wouldn't sell any of his vacation homes or his aircraft because he didn't want his friends or associates to know he was experiencing financial challenges. He felt it would damage his image and status in the community. The only property he would sell was the investment property we listed on Martha's Vineyard, and that would have a marginal effect on his situation. His future was predictable. He could easily afford his lifestyle when the market conditions were favorable, but now those conditions were working against him. Barry's jet was ultimately grounded, and the lenders foreclosed on all his other assets. He lost everything and had to rely on the generosity of a close friend to protect him from losing his home. When the situation dictates it, part of being responsible requires that you take appropriate action. Don't let your ego overrule rational decisions.

It takes time and proper care to heal from any type of injury, including a financial injury. There will be good days and bad days. It is a natural healing process that cannot be accelerated, but you must take steps forward every day or you will regress into apathy, anger, or other conditions that are counterproductive to a complete recovery. A financial failure can happen to anyone. It doesn't make you a bad person or diminish your moral character. It just means you lost money or status. The only people immune from a similar circumstance is someone who never attempted to do anything. Accept responsibility for your outcomes and don't resort to excuses to minimize the impact you are experiencing.

Taking responsibility for your thoughts is a mandatory prerequisite for success in any field of endeavor. Forcing yourself to think of success and happiness when everything around you is reflecting failure is quite difficult, to be sure. Henri Nouwen, the theologian and philosopher, likened the mind to a banana tree filled with monkeys jumping up and down, trying to get our attention. During the early days of Internet marketing, it wasn't uncommon to see a graphic of his vision blinking on and off the screen with monkeys everywhere. I have to admit, they got my attention many times, and I clicked the link to view the attached ad. This is how random thoughts of failure and discouragement infiltrate the mind. You allow them to take precedence over thoughts of success and happiness.

On a fishing trip to cousin Joey's camp one summer, my son Tommy was put in charge of the marshmallows for later consumption at the end of the day. The campfire was finally ready to start roasting our fluffy little treats when Tommy reached into his pocket to retrieve the marshmallows and pulled a handful of night-crawlers out with them. Everyone was grossed out at the sight because we all imagined that those slimy invertebrates were burrowing their way through our dessert. Tommy assured us that they didn't get into the package and roasted and ate the first one to ease our fears. Everyone enjoyed the rest of the package without concern, but our initial aversion was an example of how we often visualize and fear things that don't even exist. You need to continuously make the effort to think of things you want, not things you don't want, or the monkeys and worms will control your future.

Your subconscious mind will follow the road paved by the thoughts your conscious mind holds. If it's a confused road with many doubts and fears, you can assume the outcome will be negative and disastrous. If you hold on to thoughts of success and achievement, the road will be paved through a beautiful countryside with a feeling that everything is going your way. Evangelist Joel Osteen, one of the most positive people I know, affirmatively said that when negative thoughts stray into his mind, he immediately deletes them. "Just like a computer, delete, delete!" Even with his enormous success, he recognizes the danger of the uncontrolled negative thoughts.

For those of you who may have engaged in unprincipled behavior resulting in a failed career, business, or partnership, taking responsibility demands that you reconcile your actions with others you have injured before you can expect the freedom to improve your own circumstances. It is imperative that you do not repeat these activities, or you will be destined to join the ranks of Charles Ponzi, Bernie Madoff,

Kenneth Lay, and Jordan Belfort, the Wolf of Wall Street. All are notorious criminals indicted for fraud, deceit, money laundering, and various other charges and sentenced to many years in prison. Ill-gotten wealth never lasts. The natural law of reciprocity always has the upper hand, and you will pay the price for any nefarious deeds. If you are in this category, the responsible action is to satisfy all the damages, clean up your act, and join the ranks of those who do it right. They are the preferred fraternity if you desire bona fide success and true happiness and joy in your lifetime. As Oscar Wilde pointed out, "Every saint has a past, and every sinner has a future." Starting over from this category is a little more demanding but certainly worth the effort. No excuses. Starting today, do it right. Integrity should not be just another word in your vocabulary; it should be your way of life.

You are stronger than your current problems. No matter what has happened to you, take responsibility for your future starting right now, and do what you have to do. As Brian Tracy reminded me on my awakening night, "No one is coming to the rescue. If it's to be, you have to do it."

EXCUSES

*"Ninety-nine percent of all failures come from people who
have a habit of making excuses."*
—George Washington Carver

EXCUSES ARE LIKE STANDS OF TREES in the forest blocking
the view of the mountains beyond. Similarly, excuses stop
you from clearly seeing your future because they distract
your view of the path back to success and happiness. On a
Labor Day weekend, my youngest daughter and I went on a
road trip to western Pennsylvania to visit Falling Waters, the
remarkable house Frank Lloyd Wright had designed for one
of his clients. It is located in an area primarily populated by
family farms. Every hilltop seemed to have a few strands of
trees left, whereas all the rest of the fields had been cleared.
I learned that early farmers always left a few trees standing
alone where they would be subjected to high winds, sun, rain,

cold and heat, without protection from the other trees in the forest. This created the strongest and most valuable lumber because those trees could withstand significant stress. That lumber was used for the finest furniture, tillers, axles, and wheels and the best of the best for post and beam construction. If you feel alone and beat-up today, take some comfort in knowing that it's making you stronger. Shed the excuses. They may offer some comfort but will always stop you from becoming your strongest and most resilient self.

One of the more difficult situations, which was inherent in the entertainment agency business, is to know when people are telling the truth. For example, a bandleader of a non-exclusive act could accept an assignment from our agency while continuing to talk to other agents trying to solicit a higher paying gig for the same week. If he were successful, he would cancel our assignment. Most of the time, we satisfied our needs internally, but when we couldn't, we would gamble on a freelance act. Unfortunately, a "no show" could mean no entertainment at a venue that normally provides music for dancing or as part of a dinner-and-show package. It's a stressful situation, along with many others that could be avoided if we could be certain that the information we were given was accurate.

One day, I saw an ad for a voice stress analyzer that could be attached to your phone. The manufacturer claimed that you could detect instantly if someone was telling the truth.

The device, they promised, would beep and blink if the person you were talking with was lying. I ordered it immediately. At dinner that night, I was very excited to mention this to Carol. We discussed it for quite a while. She felt it might be good or bad, depending on the circumstances. It was going to take six to eight weeks for delivery. I eagerly anticipated putting it into service.

The following Sunday, the entire family was packed and ready for a trip to the lake when the phone rang. This was before cell phones and caller ID were available. We forwarded calls to the home phone on weekends. We had to answer it. The call was from the manager of one of our hotel clients who wanted to schedule a meeting later that day, while the regional director was in the area. I knew I couldn't make the meeting, so I began telling a story that sounded really convincing when my daughter Carrie-Ann started circling the center island in the kitchen making beep beep, beep beep sounds. I put my hand over the receiver several times to block her disruptive behavior, but she continued to beep. Finally, when I hung up the phone, I asked her, "What the heck are you doing? That call was stressful enough without all your beeping!"

"You were telling a lie, Dad. I was just doing what your new machine is going to do."

She was right! I was telling a lie because the simple truth didn't seem like an appropriate excuse for missing such an important meeting. Why am I relating this story? It's because I want you to hear beep beep, beep beep in your head every time you start with another excuse. Every time you believe you have to explain yourself to someone else, I want you to stop taking solace from your justifications of what happened to you. Live in the present! Take the beating and move on. Forget the excuses. No one is really interested, anyway.

I canceled the order for the analyzer after this event because I believe that trust and understanding is more valuable than a technical advantage when interacting with people. Especially after realizing that I also participate in lying when I perceive it to be a better choice than a potentially more damaging truth.

TIME

"Nothing is worth more than this day."
—Johann Wolfgang von Goethe

ONE OF THE NEW RESPONSIBILITIES I inherited after Carol was homebound due to her deteriorating medical condition was grocery shopping. Even as a kid shopping with my mother, the only items I ever picked were quasi-food items such as ice cream, candy bars, snacks, magazines, and an occasional box of fig squares or brownies. As an adult, that didn't change. Many times, at checkout, Carol would pick up an item I had put in the cart and, with an eye roll and heavenly stare, would murmur "Really?" as she reluctantly placed my contribution on the conveyor for purchase.

When I started shopping for both of us, however, we agreed that my food selection system wasn't working very well. She remarked on several occasions that there was no food in the house, even though I had gone shopping the previous day. Since I obviously didn't know what to buy, it was decided that Carol would make a list for me every shopping day. Even the list presented occasional problems because many products were available with several options. Thank God for cell phones to help navigate the process; otherwise, it would have caused many return trips to the market for corrective purchases.

One typical Saturday morning, Carol asked for the notepad and pen to write the weekly grocery list. After loading the trash for the transfer station, a chore that is done on the way to the market, I picked up the list she had compiled. It had only two selections.

"Where is the rest of the list?" I inquired.

"It's still in the pen," she explained apologetically.

I knew she wasn't feeling very well that day, so I didn't press the issue and headed to the grocery store without my safety net. While shopping, the thought of the list still being in the pen started resonating with me. Like a stuck song, I couldn't purge her apology from my mind. Carol was fully competent and capable of writing a grocery list, but her limited energy level and complications from her condition made it too difficult for her to complete a simple task. A week earlier, she had completed the list without effort. Now it was different and very difficult. Time started taking away her options, not just for the grocery list, but for many other choices as well.

As Shakespeare eloquently put it, "Time and Tide wait for no man." "It's still in the pen." All that was needed that day was the ability to transfer ink into cohesive words on the notepad, but time wouldn't wait. Carol's illness made it very difficult to control her productive moments. However, if you are healthy and capable of implementing changes in your life, letting time control you will produce the same results. This is why you must control your time while you still can, especially when starting over over 50. Get moving right now, not sometime in the future. Otherwise, everything you want will always be in the future, but never a reality in the present.

The power of time, choice, and focus cannot be overstated. All the money in the world cannot buy you yesterday. Waiting for conditions to be perfect will never happen either. My grandmother once told me, "If you keep waiting for the big band, you'll miss the parade." Old world wisdom, but still relevant today. She understood the concept of time, choice, and focus, without the need to define it.

Our choice line runs concurrently with our timeline. Time will ultimately end all activity. Everyone has an arrival date, and everyone will have a departure date. Our timeline is the space between those two dates. Focus points us to the right decisions during our timeline. No one on the planet has more than 24 hours each day, and yet some people accomplish far more than seems possible. It always reverts to the simple choices we have control over. If you spend your time without a goal-oriented focus, no destination of value will ever be reached. It's a ship without a rudder, drifting in an endless sea, reaching only random ports of call or ultimately crashing on the rocks.

"If I only knew then what I know now" is just another decision-delaying lament because you really do know. You have more accumulated knowledge now than at any other time in your life. If you are still casting shadows, it's not too late. You have the power to choose winning instead of apathy. Focus on the right destination and you will reach a place of success, happiness, and fulfillment. You have only so much time to choose because, just as it impacted Carol, time begins to eliminate choices. The alternative option of doing nothing to change the status quo is not a good choice. Continued indifference promulgates feelings of hopelessness, anger, depression, and—in extreme cases but not all that uncommon—suicide. Why would anyone choose to do nothing when they have a path to success within them right now? Find it and follow it to the winning side of life and experience all the requisite benefits of success, happiness, and joy.

CHOICES

"Two roads diverged in a wood, and I—
I took the one less traveled by,
And that has made all the difference."
—Robert Frost

IT HAS BEEN SAID THAT WE BECOME the sum total of our choices. The most important of all the Essential Common Denominators of Success is choice. Why? Because it is the root of all other outcomes, the driver of the bus. As each of the other Essential Common Denominators of Success is discussed, the influence of choice becomes apparent. The great news is that, to a large extent, we have control over our choices and therefore our outcomes.

When we think of choices, we tend to think of life-changing choices, such as choosing a significant other, having children, deciding upon a career, relocating to a new area, selecting a college, purchasing a house, or joining the military. Certainly, these can be life-changing decisions, but they pale in comparison to the small and seemingly inconsequential choices we make several times a day. For example, do you wake up an hour earlier and exercise, or do you need the extra hour of sleep because you chose to watch a little too much TV or socialized longer than prudent the night before? Did you take the extra glass of wine that you knew would put you over your limit? Did you choose to surf the web and invest your time in social media instead of finishing the report? Buy a new car when your finances were strained? Call out your associate or spouse because you were having a bad day and needed to feel in control? Went to a sporting event and skipped a work-related or educational seminar that could enhance your existing knowledge base in your field of endeavor? Choices are like bricks paving the road of your life. Better choices make better roads.

Doing nothing is a choice. If you don't make a choice, fate will choose one for you. A definition of insanity, often attributed to Albert Einstein, is doing the same thing over and over but expecting a different result. Instead, why not make the decision to invest the time and energy necessary to set new goals and initiate the steps required to accomplish them?

It's the everyday choices that pave the path we travel. The big decision is usually the result of hundreds of small choices that lead us to that decision crossroad. It's all about choice.

Small, easy choices can lead to great accomplishments. Most are within our control. Successful people make many small decisions every day that direct them to their destination. Consider making just one extra good decision a day. In a year, you will have accumulated 365 additional good choices. Imagine the impact on the quality of your life with an extra 365 good decisions annually.

One summer, I took my grandson on his first major hike. It included two 4,500-foot peaks and a 5,200-foot peak in the White Mountains of northern New Hampshire. At the base camp there was a map of the different trails available to the summits. My grandson chose the Falling Waters Trail for the assent. It was moderately difficult but offered spectacular scenery that included mountain streams and waterfalls at several of the trail crossings. It was a hard climb but worth the effort. Our destination was the ridgeline connecting the three mountaintops. We made it. It took hours to get there; however, we only had a few minutes to absorb the view and begin the descent before daylight turned to moonlight. On a bluff almost at the end of the hike, my grandson looked back in amazement and said, "I can't believe we were up there," pointing to the highest peak, "and we never got lost."

So simple! We had a goal. The trail was well marked, although we did make many adjustments along the way to avoid washouts and take advantage of the expansive views.

And yes, it was one step at a time. I couldn't resist explaining to my grandson that the same rules apply to everything in life.

It's the small, everyday choices that really matter. The ones we have almost total control over. Saint Augustine said, "You aspire to great things? Begin with little ones." Set your goals, take one step at a time, and don't waste too much time looking at the view or you'll be hiking in the dark. Starting over over 50 demands your full-time attention because there will be fewer big decisions if you don't. Time will end up making the decisions for you.

Your choices will determine whether your future will be relegated to telling stories of past successes to anyone willing to listen to them or of enjoying your latest accomplishments. You get to choose.

THE STATUS QUO

ONE OF THE FACTORS that tripped me and my partner up at the summit of our careers was standing on our mountaintop too long. There is a difference between persistence and stupidity. It cost our production company more to produce our commercials than we were collecting, leading to inevitable failure. We were on the wrong side of the market cycle. Advertising agencies at that time were retracting and buying low-cost productions or doing the work in-house. We were producing high-quality and high-cost music and voice-over productions at a substantial loss. We loved doing what we were doing. We were proud of our awarded work. We chose to stay the course no matter how far off course we were. We were letting our egos dictate the direction of the company instead of rational thinking. In our case, the status quo produced a failed business and mountains of debt.

Maintaining the status quo is as impossible for individuals as it is for the largest corporation. Doing nothing is a plan to fail. Just look at nature. Some days are so beautiful that we wish we could preserve them forever, but nature will have none of it. Things change. Competition will conquer the biggest players in any industry if they are not responding to the innovations or customer demands on the horizon. Starting over over 50 doesn't exempt you from the requirement of planning your future moves rather than being subjected to the conditions of that day.

One of the junkyard dealers in our area related a story to me about his father, the founder of the facility:

> Dad recognized the value in old classic auto parts. He spent well above average for Mustang, Camaro, Challenger, GTO, and other classic American muscle car parts because he believed that someday they would be very desirable. He could have sold many of these parts three times over, but he hoarded them instead, waiting for the super-premium prices he had anticipated.

Unfortunately, many manufacturers that provided replacement parts to the original auto manufactures recognized the value in those classic parts also. They started remanufacturing the original parts at very reasonable prices. They distributed them to dealers in key locations around the country for quick delivery. "Every now and then, a true purest will purchase the original part, but most buyers would rather have the new parts," the junk dealer told me. The extraordinary investment his dad made in the old parts was still causing cash flow problems years later. The status quo was a prescription for failure. "If dad had realized that competition was just over the horizon with higher quality parts and lower costs, his business would have been eminently more successful."

Don't accept the status quo unless you are very, very happy with your current position in life and able to react to changing conditions as they occur. It's easy to believe that you're locked into your present circumstances because you don't think you have the resources or the opportunity to make a different decision. The fact is, you do have the resources if you look hard enough and work with what you have. It is usually much more than we generally realize.

Helen Keller became deaf, blind, and mute after a serious illness when she was two years old, but that didn't stop her from becoming an inspiration to millions of other individuals around the world. Most people with hearing and vision never accomplish anything rivaling her achievements in education, writing, and social activism. She was missing some of her senses but found success and happiness making the most of what she had. She found a way to triumph over adversity.

Putting Adversity in Perspective

The more enlightened humans have become, the more we

realize that everything in nature is interconnected, and we are part of that connection. A recent article about fires in the Everglades explained how nature rebuilds after what appears to be a catastrophic event. The National Park Service had for years managed and controlled fires within the park through trial and error, until they realized that wildfires were an important part of the Everglades' ecological system. They recognized that fire eliminates many invasive species of plants and flora that cause damage to the native vegetation. Tree nuts crack under intense heat, releasing millions of new seeds that create the next generation of trees to replace the older or diseased specimens. In the same way, damaging habits, destructive relationships, mundane physical surroundings, and boring daily routines can be very detrimental to growth and we can benefit from the fire of change. Letting go of unproductive ways and replacing them with new possibilities can burn a path to the ultimate success and happiness you're trying to secure.

Moving out of an entrenched comfort zone can also provide opportunities not apparent from within it. Just like the Everglades, we may have allowed intrusions into our lives that damage our ambitions and camouflage the most advantageous choices we should be making. In the heat of the moment, it may appear that the fire is winning, but in the end, with the right attitude, it will be a blessing. The fire in my own life exposed flawed decision-making habits and assumptions based on incomplete data. It also made me realize that I should rely on my gut feelings, because they have always pointed me in the right direction. Whenever I overruled my inner voice, trouble always followed. Sound familiar?

FIND THE OPEN DOOR

*"When one door closes, another is opened.
Nature never takes anything away without replacing
it with something of equal or greater value"*
—Anonymous

ONE OF THE INDIANA JONES MOVIES has a scene where Indy and his father are on an open beach being attacked by an enemy airplane firing its machine gun at the two of them. As they are preparing for a second and probably fatal encounter with the plane, Indy takes out his handgun in hopes he can make a one in a million shot and disable the aircraft. Unfortunately, when he checks his ammo, the chambers are empty. He becomes frozen in his tracks, believing the outcome is hopeless. Right at that moment, his father begins running down the beach toward the incoming airplane, opening and closing his umbrella and screaming as loud as he can. Indy assumes his father is in the process of losing his mind. However, Dad's ranting causes thousands of seabirds to become aroused and take flight. They collide with the plane, causing it to lose control and crash into a ridge overlooking the perimeter of the beachfront. The umbrella is much more effective than the gun. It's only a movie, but the writer understood the basic principle that while you're still casting shadows, you are never without options.

Another Open Door

The hospital environment is not very conducive to inspiration either for the patient or the caregiver. It's an endless litany of tests, infusions, x-rays, nurses, orderlies, doctors, and administrators. Hours and hours become days and days of a routine that can wear out even the most positive personality. During one of Carol's many protracted hospital stays, my capacity to go with the flow reached a maximum frustration point. I felt like I was a patient also. My business was severely impacted, and my ability to remedy that situation from the hospital room was almost impossible. The options to change the status quo appeared to be very limited.

The facility was a huge complex with multiple floors and plenty of corridors open to public passage. While Carol was sleeping, I started walking every corridor and level many times daily. On one such occasion, I recalled how many years earlier I wanted to write a book that related true stories about everyday people that discovered the common denominators to success; common because every success story includes these principles. The book would be composed of interviews with many successful people to serve as a roadmap for the reader to follow. It was to be titled The Essential Common Denominators of Success. It was never written because I did not choose to commit the time and focus to make it happen. However, why not now? Why not while I was captive in an environment with little to do but watch others doing their job? This was my incentive to start this book. It was an open door when every other door was rapidly closing. My despair became hope. Hope that I could make use of this time in a productive and rewarding way. All I needed was a laptop and the inspiration to get started.

Since I couldn't interview people in the hospital room, I turned the focus of this book to my own personal experiences to demonstrate how anyone, even after the age of 50, can regroup and reframe their life in a powerful and proactive way to achieve success and happiness later in life. It doesn't just happen to other people. Doors are available for you to go through; there are ways around any challenging circumstances you may encounter. There are no dead ends, only your choice to stop looking.

THE POWER OF
THOUGHTS

*"Think you can, think you can't, either way you
will be right."* —Henry Ford

IRREFUTABLE EVIDENCE, ACCUMULATED from hundreds of
controlled studies, substantiates that the power of thought,
positive thinking, and visualization does influence the degree of success and happiness we will attain. In a Harvard
University study, half of a group of individuals with equal
intellect and age were asked to start playing piano and practice scales several times a day. The other half of the group
was asked to only visualize playing the same scales several
times a day. Their brains were scanned before and after the
testing period. Remarkably, the part of the brain associated

with dexterity of the fingers, such as playing piano, showed significant development in both groups.

Additional research has confirmed the association of happy thoughts and positive thinking with higher degrees of contentment, achievement, and longer life. Why would anyone think anything but happy thoughts? The real answer is that it takes a degree of concentration and effort to gradually align your thinking with positive and meaningful thoughts. Everything worthwhile takes some effort. Left unattended, negative thoughts will rule the day the same way weeds grow in the garden without any provocation. Stress, fear, anxiety, and worry consume more time and energy than almost any other factors when trying to stabilize a foundation to rebuild your financial condition, career, relationships or status. Real and imagined obstacles can become overwhelming if we allow them the space to propagate.

The only way to combat the impact these conditions have on you is to eliminate them entirely. I know, it sounds impossible especially when you're the one experiencing these conditions. The trick is to put them into perspective. Jesus once said, *"Can any one of you by worrying add a single hour to your life?"* A relevant question even today. Since your mind can only hold one thought at a time, the best weed killer is to have positive visions that can be summoned when destructive thoughts of fear and doubt creep in—for example, a vision of how it will feel to achieve your goals, the recognition, the pride of accomplishment, and the freedom that money can provide. Replace fear with visions of the happiness and joy you will experience when sharing quality time with family and friends as they congratulate you on your successes. Vividly imagine commanding mountains or valley vistas and seashores; they will have a calming effect. The idea is to have these preplanned vignettes ready for action when the need arises. Through the power of choice, you will have the upper hand and decide what you will allow in your conscious mind.

Another astonishing fact demonstrated time and time again is that visualization is one of the most powerful tools for achievement in all categories of life, and we are in complete control of this awesome power. Many top athletes have stated that they won their greatest victories in the mind long before they took to the field or court to physically experience their triumph. Michael Jordan, Tiger Woods, and Carli Lloyd all use visualization. Jim Carrey, the actor, carried a $10,000,000 check in his wallet, made out to him, with a memo that stated, "Acting services rendered." He was struggling at the time he wrote this check, but 10 years later he was paid $10,000,000 for his role in Dumb and Dumber. Coincidentally, the check in his wallet was dated 10 years from the date it was written. Oprah Winfrey recommends, "Create the highest and grandest vision possible for your life, because you become what you believe." Arnold Schwarzenegger used this power for his body-building success, his acting career, and later in political life to visualize his victory as governor of California.

One way to activate this endowment is a visualization board. When I decided to do something other than smoke, I created a poster board with images of the benefits I would realize when I replaced smoking with other activities. It included a painting of a crisp, clear morning with brilliant beams of sunshine illuminating a mountain and valley scene. A photo of a handsome, physically fit man with clear eyes and an ear-to-ear smile, a runner winning a race by a formidable distance over his closest contender, and a group of happy couples having fun without anyone smoking. A sticky note describing myself as a non-smoking, highly fit, successful individual was pasted at the bottom of the board along with a six-month chart of progress to track how I was doing at the end of each month. It worked perfectly! Whenever I was experiencing a weak moment, I would look at my poster board to remind myself of why I was on this mission. I have never had a cigarette since the day I chose that path. I credit my victory over smoking to the power of visualizing the alternative.

Don't underestimate the power of the mind. Many studies have confirmed that habits are learned events. Philosopher Will Durant concluded, "Excellence is not an act, but a habit." Of all the learned habits, the first in line should be the habit of positive thinking about today, your future, your health, your relationships, and your success and happiness. Whether it takes 21 days or 500 days to form these habits, it is worth every effort. Since you're going to put the time in anyway, why not put the time in deliberately programming the way you think? You can never break an old habit by sheer willpower. This is why most diets or alcohol and drug abuse programs don't work. You need to visualize an alternative to replace the old behavior, so that the old behavior is no longer compatible with who you want to be. You are your own fortune teller. Start with a visualization board of what you want by posting pictures of the individuals and quotes that inspire you. Include inserts of houses, cars, fashions, vacation destinations, and bank-account balances. Fitness goals should be high on the list because they affect both our mental and physical health. Look at it first thing in the morning and as often as possible during the day to reinforce your intentions. The board can be a digital display on your computer or a physical board, such as my alternative to smoking board. You can have multiple boards to thoroughly cover all the habits, people, and physical needs you intend to attract. Starting is always the hardest part, but once in process, you are activating some of the most powerful tools in the universe, your imagination, and the unlimited potential we all have available to us. When organized thought and intense emotions are activated together, you're unstoppable.

FOCUS AND TRAINING

"Do not lower your goals to the level of your abilities.
Instead, raise your abilities to the height of your goals."
—Swami Vivekananda

RANDOM THOUGHTS OF FAILURE AND discouragement will disrupt your focus if you allow them the opportunity to occupy your thinking. This is an area you have complete control over. You need to continuously make the effort to focus on what you want, not what you don't want. This can only be accomplished in the present. Focus on the steps, not the distance. If you're on the right path, sooner or later you will end up at your destination. Believe in yourself and your goals. Picture what you want and move past things you cannot control such as how someone else thinks or the weather. You can never be successful chasing things beyond your control. Focus instead on your goals and the preparations necessary to move your plans forward.

When I was in high school it was a requirement that every student join at least two extracurricular activities. I joined the debating society and the yearbook club, but I also wanted to do an athletic activity. I tried out for hockey, but those guys from French Hill were much better skaters than I could ever hope to be. Football didn't work either. After being crushed on the ground several times during the first day of practice, the coach pretty much told me that football would not be in my future. One of my teachers recommended that I go out for cross country running. *That sounds good to me,* I thought.

On the first day, we all met at the top of a hill located a short distance from our school. The coach indicated we should all start running on the first street and spotters would direct us to the correct turns on the course. I ran about a quarter-mile when a pain in my side nearly crippled me. I walked the balance of the route and finished dead last. The coach told me I would do better tomorrow.

When tomorrow came, I ran a little farther than the day before, but not by much. Our first meet came a week later. I had never tried harder at anything than I did that day. About a mile into the race, the same crippling pain took over again, and I finished dead last out of the three schools in attendance. How is that possible? I never had any difficulty keeping up with any kids in my neighborhood. Why now?! Nearly in tears, I asked the coach what I should do. Find another sport was the expected answer.

Instead he asked, "How much do you train?"

"What do you mean train?! How do you train for running?"

"How many miles did you run this week, before today?" he asked.

"No miles! I don't understand what you are getting at."

"You can't expect to show up on Saturday morning and run a good race if you haven't been training. That means practice running, muscle development, and performance goals. If you don't train most days, you can never expect to compete on race day."

Can you believe it?! Train to run! If a bear or bad guy was chasing me, I'd run! Who would ever believe that you need to train to do something as basic as run?

The lesson that day was that no amount of trying can ever compete with preparation. This simple lesson has come back many times during my life. When I started the real estate agency, I realized that research was the key. Knowing as much as we possibly could assemble about the person or persons we were to meet, what their likely criteria would be, and how we could assist them all became paramount steps to success. It wouldn't be uncommon to commit three to four hours of research time for every 30 minutes in front of the client. There is not a person involved in a successful career who has not invested the amount of time necessary to learn the job well enough to get it done right. Top doctors, lawyers, teachers, politicians, mechanics, engineers, contractors, athletes, and virtually every other profession has its star participants. As a musician, I should have known this. It took years of practice to become a reasonably good stage performer. Buying a guitar, but never practicing, makes you a collector, not a musician. Focus and preparation separate the successful individuals from the dreamers.

We may not want to think of it this way, but we have spent our entire life training for where we are now. If you're happy, the training paid off. If you are not satisfied with your position in life, then either your training was flawed, or your goals were not clear enough for the training to be effective. For example, if you never attended a class or opened a book on law, how could you possibly expect to be a great attorney? You may have had the right goal, but your training was very flawed. If on the other hand you spent your life studying law and became a successful lawyer but are unhappy, perhaps it was your goal that was flawed. In Steven Covey's book, *The 7 Habits of Highly Effective People*, he mentions climbing the ladder of success only to find that the ladder is leaning on the wrong wall. If you're starting over over 50, don't let the excuse of age interfere with making a different decision. If your ladder is on the wrong wall, move the ladder.

An old Chinese proverb says, *"The best time to plant a tree was 20 years ago. The second-best time to plant a tree is today."* Don't live another day of your life without identifying and focusing on what will make you happy and successful, and then prepare to get there. Every sunset is the end of another day of opportunity. We all have the same 24 hours, and how we choose to use them will determine how much we will enjoy the sunset.

FAITH AND BELIEF

*"Ask and it will be given to you, seek and you will find,
knock and the door will be opened for you."* —Jesus

It seems so abstract to think that by just believing good
things will happen, they will. However, my own personal
experiences have shown me that this is the case. The Hopi
Indians say it best: *"Believe it and you will see it."* Not the
other way around, as is so often recited. Here are two of the
many examples I can relate to from my own experiences.

Our New Home

When our family moved to the rental property it was a difficult adjustment. Not only was it on a dead-end street, but
it backed up to the largest cemetery in the area. There wasn't
any grass—it was more of a gravel lot. It was a significant

change from the professionally landscaped surroundings and numerous amenities of our previous residence.

One of my written goals on my "awakening night" was to be in a new house within four years. Carol and I had never built a new house, but we always wanted the opportunity to design and construct one. After looking at many plan books over the years I knew exactly the type of house we should build. I copied the two most logical plans and printed large renderings of the two choices. I placed both of them on the refrigerator and told Carol and my daughter Kristi to pick the one they liked best. They would have to look at the pictures every time they went into the refrigerator. They both thought I was crazy considering our circumstances. I wouldn't relent. I constantly asked them if they had made a decision. A few months into the process they both decided on a plan. It was a plan that provided plenty of living space without wasting space. We modified the plan to include cathedral ceilings, an expansive archway, and other architectural details to make it uniquely ours.

The three of us would look at vacant lots almost every Sunday after church trying to find the right place to build our future dream home. Nothing seemed to truly spark our interest. We all preferred our previous address. There was a single lot remaining in our old neighborhood owned by one of the wealthiest residents of our community. He lived on one of the lots and had purchased an extra lot for privacy 20 years earlier. We drove by it continually during our search and visualized how we would place the house behind an overgrown area in the front. Kristi wanted to keep the vegetation because she had spotted many small animals living there, including a family of rabbits, a groundhog, and a woodpecker in one of the dead trees. She referred to it as the animal condominium.

Most of the neighbors, including me, believed that the owner would never sell the lot because he certainly didn't need the money and his privacy would be compromised to some degree if he did. Both Carol and Kristi wanted to live in the old neighborhood, so did I, but I knew that would be impossible. Carol wasn't so sure, and after months of looking at lots she decided to meet with our former neighbor. She really believed that he would sell the lot to us regardless of the consensus of opinion in the neighborhood. When she returned from the meeting, she announced that he would love to have us as neighbors again.

I couldn't believe it! Ten people a year must have asked him about his land, and he refused all of them. Why us? "Believe it and you will see it." Fortunately, Carol's beliefs were much stronger than mine when it came to the possibility of acquiring that specific lot. She just wanted to live there and nowhere else. I attended the next meeting and we signed an offer at a very reasonable price. Although the agency was doing quite well, we didn't have all the money yet, so our neighbor provided us with a satisfactory window to accumulate the additional funds. A few months later, we closed on the lot and started construction on our dream home, almost exactly in the time period envisioned in my written goals on the awakening night.

The $4.5 Million Golf Ball

My son Rob always wanted to be wealthy. Even as a kid he was attracted to large homes, fast cars, and other perks that rich people enjoyed. He started golfing at a fairly young age and liked the concept of living at a golf course community someday with other successful businessmen. He has an extroverted personality, is very articulate, and can develop a rapport with almost anyone.

Rob's first full-time job after college was working at a major bank in Boston, where he was part of the bank's real estate team. His department was responsible for marketing large commercial properties that the bank had repossessed during the real estate meltdown in the early '90s. It was the same meltdown that absorbed all the value from my commercial real estate holdings. Later, he became a site selector for national organizations. He was responsible for identifying locations and negotiating leases for cell towers, bagel shops, and fast-food restaurants.

One of the companies Rob was employed by required that he perform site selecting and manage franchisee relationships within his assigned territory. He observed that many operators were not very knowledgeable about their business, and in some cases, they didn't understand the methods and procedures needed to increase sales and garner greater customer loyalty. Rob enjoyed helping his clients become better operators; however, after years of helping others become successful, Rob's goal was to open his own stores. He was ready. This takes a significant amount of money because each store can cost upwards of $1 million to build or renovate, inventory, staff, advertise, and open. Rob recognized that developing a single store at a time would not be the best plan to become a multi-store operator, which was his goal. His accumulated experiences and knowledge qualified him to think much bigger.

Rob's number-one problem was that he didn't have the money. I certainly couldn't help him at that time, and although he did fairly well while working with these various companies, saving beyond average living expenses was difficult. He recognized that if he was going to accomplish something remarkable, he would need to find an investor partner. During the next few years, he talked to several people who were capable of helping him, but none of them stepped up to finance his ambitions. Somewhat frustrated, but not giving up on his goals, he continued to look for the right person.

Rob eventually moved to a golf course community, the

dream he had visualized many years earlier. On the course one day, he hit a bad shot that went off the fairway and landed in the backyard of one the abutters to the golf community. The owner of the home happened to notice him retrieving the golf ball and said hi. After striking up a conversation, they decided to meet at the clubhouse later to just talk about business in general.

During the meeting, his neighbor disclosed he had recently sold his software business and was looking for a new venture. Rob presented him with his plan to develop a multi-store operation within his assigned territory as a master franchisee of the fast-food concept. Not being shy, Rob told him he would need $4.5 million over time to make the company work. By the end of the meeting his new acquaintance became his investor partner and eagerly fronted the start-up funds for the first restaurant. Within a few years they owned and operated six locations, all producing a sales volume exceeding national averages within the company. They were well run and profitable, and the partner received a significant return on his investment.

To many, Rob seemed to find overnight success, but this is not the case. It was the culmination of many years of learning his trade and developing plans that prepared him for that chance encounter with his investor. It is a classic example of perspiration meeting opportunity. Rob's passionate belief that if he worked hard and planned properly, he would achieve his goals demonstrates again that faith in your mission, and persistence, will lead you to your destination. Situations that seem impossible just occur. In the '60s, they called it serendipity; others call it luck. It doesn't really matter how you define it; it absolutely works!

SOW AND REAP

"What you sow, you are entitled to reap,
nothing less, nothing more." —Anonymous

THE HOUSING PROJECT WHERE WE grew up was on a hill
in the middle of nowhere at the time. It was probably built
there because the land was cheap and abutter resistance
would be very low. One advantage, however, was that it
was surrounded by dense woods in every direction. Many
exciting summer adventures took place in those beautiful
and mysterious woods. My brother Michael and I were
regular explorers. Whatever we read in a *Classic's Illustrated*
comic or viewed at the movies or on TV would usually spark
our next adventure. If it wasn't inspired by Disney's series
about Davy Crockett or Daniel Boone, it would be from a
Saturday matinee featuring a John Wayne western or some
other movie depicting a plethora of possible undertakings.

On one such occasion, our intention was to head into the woods in search of small saplings to cut into spears. We had just seen a movie where the Indians had used their lances with great precision, producing a favorable ending to their plight. We had done this before with dead branches, but today was different. We were on a hunt for the straightest and best spears we could find. We were going across the avenue to the largest forest in the area to find our treasure.

We picked up some dead branches as usual and carved a point with our knives. Almost everyone had a small jack-knife in those days. It was a part of growing up. I had a Boy Scout version that featured two blades, long and short, that folded into the monogrammed bone handle. Michael wasn't a Boy Scout, so he had a recycled steak knife with a wooden handle that he slipped between his belt and trousers. We were following the well-worn paths that twisted in and around the center of the woods when we came upon a clump of small maple saplings. This was it! Eight of the straightest, ideal diameter spears we've ever seen. They were live trees so snapping the stock was very difficult. I decided to carve a point at the end of one sapling, making it easier to break off. Michael came up with a considerably easier plan.

"This entire clump is loose," he said, "All we have to do is lean on the branches, back and forth a few times, and we can get all the spears out together."

Wow, what an idea! We could take the entire clump back

home. Then we would both have four perfect spears each that we could carve as we needed them. It was like hitting the mother lode! The jackpot! So little work for such a big payoff!

"I'll lean toward you and then you push them back to me," Michael said excitedly.

We did the back and forth exercise until the clump was finally loose enough to break it away from the ground. Michael gave one last robust pull—and success! They were all out. Suddenly, I felt a sharp prick on the side of my head. As I reacted to the insult, there was another, then another. Simultaneously, Michael started screaming as he rolled on the ground flailing his hands over his head and neck. Wasps, millions of wasps were attacking us from everywhere. We both gathered enough strength to start running as fast as we could, but the persistent little pests kept stinging us until we crossed the avenue on our way back home.

Michael ended up in the hospital that night with more than a hundred stings. I lucked out with only 20 or so. Not enough for a hospital stay but enough to never forget the lesson learned that day. Although it was a little more work, if we had carved just the one spear at a time that we needed instead of trying to hit the jackpot, we wouldn't have exposed the wasp nest. Maybe a few bees would have taken exception to our intrusion but certainly not the entire wasp civilization.

There are no shortcuts to success and expecting great rewards from a small effort is usually fraught with disappointment. Rob's chance encounter with his investor, referenced earlier, was preceded by years of sowing before he reaped any reward. Good choices will limit wasted effort and expedite the process but expecting something for nothing is stupidity. If your future retirement plan is winning the lottery, you will most probably end up broke and very disappointed. Understanding the principle of sow and reap will protect you from this potential pitfall. You must plant before you can harvest. It's that simple.

CHANGE

"It is not the strongest of the species that survives, nor the most intelligent. It is the one that is the most adaptable to change." —Charles Darwin

CHANGE IS BOTH A CURSE AND a blessing depending on how you view it. The good old days in fact were the good old days when they occurred. We can resist change and run the risk of diminishing our relevancy in the present, or we can adapt to change, recognizing that change is inevitable and embrace all the benefits of living in the present.

Consider changes just in the past 10 years at this point in history. Most of us use personal communication devices that do things that would have required a room full of Big Blue computers a generation ago. Change made it possible to carry that room in our pocket or purse. Apple became the first trillion-dollar company in the world because it thrived on change. Steve Jobs recognized that complacency in the modern world would hinder growth and innovation. As he said, "The best way to predict the future is to create it." Imagine trying to carry thousands of vinyl records or CDs and a player with you every day just so you could listen to your favorite songs. In less than one generation, Apple's innovative approach to music libraries provided access to millions of selections using our personal communication devices. What do you think happened to most of the manufacturers of vinyl records and CDs?

Not adapting to change was one of the single biggest contributors to the failure of our advertising production facility. As discussed earlier, the market was changing, and we didn't adjust to the current market conditions. If we'd had greater resources, we might have survived that difficult market, but we didn't. The right choice would have been to accept the new realities of the time by trimming our budgets and renting our facility for alternative projects. Technology was also a contributing factor. Electronic music technology allowed competitors working in very low overhead conditions the ability to deliver productions that rivaled the work created at the most expensive facilities and reduced the number of musicians needed to only a few. That change may have contributed to our failure; however, new technologies allow all of us to do in a few years what once took decades to accomplish. We have more resources available to assist us today than at any other time in human history.

Every day we are living, changes are occurring in our physical, mental, emotional, spiritual, financial, and social lives. If you are starting over over 50 you obviously need to change something, or you wouldn't be investing your time reading this book.

Change can alter circumstances almost overnight. You're rich and successful one day, the next you're homeless. Conversely, you're homeless one day, but an idea came to you that helped you to become wildly rich and successful.

You had an amazing career that is suddenly terminated by circumstances you had no control over. Conversely, you are hired by a renowned company and elevated to an upper management position with more responsibility, a much higher pay grade, and lucrative stock options.

You were the epitome of good health all of your life when suddenly a medical condition forces you to completely readjust to the new realities of your limited physical capabilities. Conversely, your medical team prescribed the right treatment, and you feel better than you have in years.

You were a great athlete, but now you're past the point where anyone will pay for your current level of performance. Conversely, your experience as an athlete qualified you for one of the highest paying and most prestigious coaching jobs in the country.

You are years away from retirement, and you can't imagine spending even one more day doing what you are doing because you're burned out. Conversely, you approach a friend with an idea that you have dreamed about for years, and he partners with you to start a new company doing something you truly enjoy, and it provides more income than you ever thought possible.

Somehow that great marriage is failing, and now you're devastated at the impact it is having on you. Conversely, you and your spouse find a way to reconcile your differences and now expect a much brighter future together than you could have ever experienced living apart.

For most people the pendulum doesn't always swing to extremes. You can go from down and out to an elevation where just your basic needs are now being met but desire more. Or you could be firmly middle class and suddenly slip below your safety net and want to return to your previous economic level. Subtle, but still very impactful.

Change! Change! Change! Without change, little would happen. This is why happy and successful people recognize that change is inevitable, and they accept it, rather than fear it. They are also aware that change most often improves circumstances and provides new opportunities. When change has a negative impact, the marines say, "Improvise, adapt, and overcome." When change is positive, be thankful and appreciate the multitude of benefits change has initiated.

Staying Relevant Over 50

Johnny M, the former lead guitar player and vocalist in my teen band, played music his entire life as his only profession and means of support. Just after finishing an engagement one night, he experienced a fatal heart attack. He had amazing talent, not only as a musician and vocalist but also as a prolific songwriter. He was thoroughly engaged in his art. The remaining members of his band, which included me and most of the local music community, hosted a memorial service for Johnny, one of its most loved and respected performers. As part of the event, we produced a compilation CD of his originals and signature cover songs. We sold almost every copy that night and donated the proceeds to his favorite charity.

A few years after Johnny's passing, I was befriended by a younger woman. One night at dinner, I discussed my musical roots and related the history of this super talent that I'd had the privilege of sharing a stage with for seven years.

"With the right opportunities, he could have been an international celebrity," I said, "but he chose to be the biggest fish in our hometown pond. That didn't diminish his talent," I assured her.

When we got into the car to head home, I was very excited to put his CD into the audio system, crank up the volume, and share these amazing tracks with her fresh ears. Halfway through the first song, she began talking over the music, discussing an entirely different subject. My thought was she wasn't really paying attention, so I introduced his next selection with enough fanfare that I was certain she would react as anticipated. However, she continued to talk about unrelated subjects no matter how often I tried to transition back to the topic at hand. I switched to live radio instead of continuing the presentation. Obviously, I was much more invested in the moment than my friend.

So, what happened? Relevance, that's what happened. His music and his story were not relevant to her that night. Great memories and great music but regardless of how talented Johnny was, her interests were in the here and now and the music styles of today. It's the same with your career endeavors. Skills are forever. Johnny could play any song ever written including contemporary styles of music with a little practice and the desire to perform the material. He had the skill to do that, but he didn't have to change his repertoire because he had a very significant following who enjoyed his older style of music. Unlike Johnny, if you are in an industry that requires change, then change. Your skills may only need updating to stay relevant as new trends develop.

Keep in mind that everyone wants to be relevant. It's normal to sometimes believe that you are losing ground to your peers or to the younger generations as you age. It's just your view of the circumstances and not an accurate evaluation. You can preserve your relevance by living in the present and committing a small amount of your time every day to learn more about developments in your profession, current events, and the new technologies that are influencing all of us. It's a small investment that really pays giant dividends when accumulated over time. My grandmother was 102 when she was admitted to the nursing home. She was still the go-to person to find out what was taking place with more than a hundred family members. That was her passion and profession. If she could remain relevant at 102, you certainly can do it if you are younger. Age has little to do with relevancy. It's a personal choice within your control. Acquiring knowledge daily is certainly easier than trying to catch up after years of indifference. Make new memories, sing new songs!

WRITE YOUR OWN SCRIPTS

"Be yourself. Everyone else is taken."
—Orson Wells

MOST OF US CAN FIND HAPPINESS and joy in our lives without the need for overwhelming financial success. If that kind of success happens, great, but if it doesn't, it certainly shouldn't be a source of unhappiness. A good life is one that is lived on your terms, with your script, not someone else's. You don't need to be rich and famous to love your family and friends or lend a helping hand to a needy neighbor. It's easy to be distracted by the images we see on TV, online, in magazines, and on the big screen of the perfect people, living in their magical kingdoms and indulging themselves in their wildest fantasies. Such as, palatial estates, exotic cars, trendy fashions, A-list parties, and vacationing on secluded private islands somewhere in the South Pacific. None of those things can bring joy and happiness without an inner peace that can come only from being content and satisfied that you are living your life to the fullest. An Easter egg hunt with your grandchildren in the backyard or a day at the beach with friends can be far more satisfying than an A-list party. Don't buy into the Hollywood scripts. They're intended to be fiction. Real life is different. You need to write your own script.

Two of the happiest and contented people I have known are my friend Dan Chan and my Uncle John.

Dan Chan

Dan Chan was one of my clients at the entertainment agency and later engaged our real estate firm when he decided to sell his commercial properties. He was the owner of two of the largest Chinese restaurants in our area. One of the better bands to play in his establishments was a group called Sunshyne, always a sell-out. One afternoon, on a set-up day, the bandleader related to me that Dan had asked them to work out a couple of songs that he wanted to sing on Saturday night. I didn't think Dan had ever sung professionally or performed anywhere in public. If he had, I'm certain it would have been a topic of conversation long before then. He was already in his late 50s when he decided to start this new chapter. He asked the bandleader to teach him how to sing "Love Me Tender," by Elvis Presley, and "You Were Always on My Mind," by Willie Nelson.

That Saturday night, I went to the restaurant to hear Dan make his debut performance. When I asked him how he felt, he said very good, just a little nervous. He said he had been practicing all week and was positive his customers would be pleased.

The place was packed as would be expected with Sunshyne performing. Around 10:30, the bandleader made the announcement that Dan Chan would be up to sing a few songs around the middle of the set. Everyone in the crowd started buzzing about this. No one knew exactly what to expect, but they were certainly looking forward to it. The bartenders and servers were equally surprised by the announcement.

Dan had two family members who worked for him, Honey and Connie. They managed the front desk and handled reservations and seating in the restaurant section of the building. When I asked them if they had heard Dan sing before, neither one of them could think of a single occasion. I asked them if they had heard him sing during rehearsal. Neither one of them worked in the afternoon, and they were unable to provide any advanced expectations.

The moment of truth finally arrived, and Dan took to the stage accompanied by thunderous applause from his patrons. He announced that this was his premier performance and that he planned to be doing this on a regular basis. The crowd again gave him another standing ovation in support of his pending performance. Finally, the song began and Dan started singing. He looked great, he had good stage presence, but he sang terribly. I was embarrassed for him. Mercifully, his two-song repertoire finally ended. The audience gave him an enthusiastic round of applause even though most were laughing hysterically at what they had just heard.

Fifteen minutes later, after he worked his way through the crowd, Dan arrived at the front desk. The first person he encountered was Connie. "Connie, what do you think?"

"Dan, you sounded like you were singing underwater. It was awful."

Not to let a single critic discourage him, he turned to Honey and asked her the same question.

"Dan, only goats would be members of your fan club. This is something you shouldn't be doing."

When he turned to me, I was fearful of how I would deal with the situation. Luckily, Dan didn't ask me what I thought but offered the following observation with a smile: "I guess I'll have to rehearse more."

Rehearse more?! Seriously?! Especially after his family's critique?! Most people would be so discouraged that they would hide in a dark closet for years before exiting.

Amazingly, rehearse more is exactly what he did. For

years he performed not only in his restaurants, but some of his competitors invited him to sing in their nightclubs also. He really didn't improve all that much from his initial performance, but he was so much fun to watch on stage, and everyone loved and respected him. "New York, New York" and "My Way" by Frank Sinatra were perennial requests from his fans. Even local politicians would invite him to their events to sing a song or two and tell a few of his humorous stories. Dan continued singing well into his 90s. Although he didn't need the money, he worked every Friday and Saturday night tending bar, telling stories, and sharing his perceptive Asian wisdom. He is one of the happiest and most respected people I've known. Dan refused to let someone else write his script. He wrote his new script in his 50s and enjoyed significant success and happiness just being himself.

Uncle John

My uncle John, on my mother's side of the family, worked as an upholsterer most of his life. Although he survived with very limited resources, he was another one of the happiest individuals I've known. He had that charisma people envy. When he walked into a room, you felt his presence even before he spoke. He was funny and intelligent. He had a way of making you feel important when he engaged you in conversation. You couldn't put your finger on it, but you just felt good being around him.

I was impressed at the number of people who attended his funeral. Why were they here for an upholsterer? The service was held at Saint Marie's in Manchester, New Hampshire, the largest church in our state. Every seat was taken. Three clergymen celebrated the Mass and a large choir filled the church with appropriate selections of music instead of the usual solo singer. I couldn't figure out what was going on. Was I at the right funeral?

During the homily, the monsignor spoke about Uncle John: "We will all miss this man. He was a loving father and husband, but more than that, he showed all of us what it means to truly serve others. His wife Annette has been in a nursing home for several years now. He has not missed a single day without having lunch with her, even though her ability to recognize anyone around her has been lost for years. That didn't matter to John, because even though his beloved Annette didn't recognize him, he certainly knew who she was. His loyalty and devotion to her is an inspiration for all of us to follow."

The monsignor then related this story about Uncle John:

Every Christmas, the nativity display with baby Jesus and all the supporting cast are sponsored by individuals from our parish. There is a lottery to determine the order of selection. Usually, the first to pick chooses to sponsor the baby Jesus figurine because the sponsorships are ranked in their order of importance. Most parishioners lovingly envy the number-one sponsor because their name is at the top of the list. It's a prestigious position to sponsor the baby Jesus, Mary, or Joseph at Christmas. When John was picked one year to make the first selection, I said to him, "I assume you want baby Jesus."

"No, not Jesus."

"Mary?"

"No, not Mary."

Surprised that he passed on the first two choices, I was certain he wanted Saint Joseph.

"Joseph is a good choice, John. He is the protector of the family."

"No, not Joseph!"

"You don't want Jesus, Mary, or Joseph. Which figurine do you want?" I asked in exasperation.

"I want to sponsor the donkey," John said.

"The donkey, you want the donkey! Why would you want the donkey?"

"Because the donkey carried the first family to Bethlehem," John replied. "Without the donkey, Mary would have had the baby out on the trail somewhere. He carried them all the way from Nazareth to that stable in Bethlehem."

"That was John," the monsignor said, "a man of service. He wasn't concerned about letting other people receive the recognition. He just carried the load for them. He was their donkey. He was the organizer of the church's reception after every funeral so that families had a place to assemble and reflect about their departed loved ones. He worked tirelessly for the St. Vincent DePaul Society in the city, he was a member of the Knights of Columbus, a regular server at the soup kitchen, and organizer of many charitable drives to support the disadvantaged in our community."

The monsignor concluded: "He was a set-up man. He took no bows, but without him, all of us here today would be diminished. Yes, John was a loving father and husband, but also a man who brought something extra to our table. May God bless and keep him."

After the service, I met with several members of his extended family in the church hall for a light lunch and a remembrance social. This was the same reception he had organized for other members of the parish. Several attendees mentioned his endless energy and willingness to go far beyond reasonable expectations in supporting his charity teams throughout the city. As one person said, "If we had millions of dollars, it wouldn't be enough to replace his contributions. I really loved that man."

Success does not need to be measured in dollars and cents. If your goal is to experience a life of happiness, joy, and contentment, it really doesn't matter what elevates you to those states of mind. For some people success in their career and the requisite financial reward provides a foundation for these higher states of being. They are a means, but certainly not an absolute for happiness, joy, and contentment. Love levels the playing field and transcends income and position. In fact, money and power often complicate the simplicity of a loving relationship. If given the choice, start with love and then seek the level of accumulation you believe will enhance your life.

Money in the right hands is also a powerful tool for elevating the human condition beyond our personal needs. When Paul Newman was near death, he remarked, "It has been such a privilege to be here." He made the most of his life as an actor, race car driver, and philanthropist. The charities he established while he was alive contributed hundreds of millions of dollars to multiple organizations and continue to fund even more today.

Bill and Melinda Gates, along with Warren Buffett, intend to donate and bequest most of their enormous wealth to world charities. They have a goal to eradicate polio proliferation and end epidemics of AIDS, tuberculosis, malaria, and other neglected tropical diseases in many impoverished parts of the world. They have provided curative drugs to tens of thousands of afflicted people, set up hospital facilities, and administered free pre and post-natal care to thousands of expecting mothers and their children in developing countries. Their efforts have already saved an untold number of lives.

Oprah Winfrey's charities have spent many millions of dollars educating and improving the lives of the disadvantaged in America and in Africa. There are literally thousands of highly successful men and women who, like her, have used their vast resources and influence to improve millions of lives on this planet we all occupy.

Although not impossible, most of us will never accumulate the wealth of these successful individuals, but all of us can contribute just as Uncle John has contributed with the single most valuable resource we have, our time. Uncle John's skills were the same skill sets that are used by most of the giants in corporate America. If Uncle John had chosen to be part of the corporate world, I'm certain he would have been much wealthier than most of his peers. He followed his own script and found success, happiness, and joy throughout his life, and on his terms. Uncle John truly understood the big picture. If he had lived a few more years, the diocese would have needed a bigger church. As Mark Twain put it, "Let us so live so that when we come to die even the undertaker will be sorry."

Your Script

Is it really possible to write a whole new script for your life if you're over 50? If you need to change, can you really change that much history? Can you regain the energy and enthusiasm of your youth and actually become the person you believed you could be? The answer to all three questions is a resounding yes, yes, yes. The number-one catalyst for all three categories is mindset—a belief, beyond fear, that you can accomplish what you envision. Consider this. Harvard University Professor Dr. Ellen Langer, who has written 11 books and hundreds of research papers, believes that the mind-body connection is irrefutable. In her book Counterclockwise, she analyzes an experiment where she placed men in their late 70s and 80s in a retrofitted environment that replicated the one these men would have experienced 20 years earlier. The participants were not allowed to talk about anything current, only about events that were 20 years old or earlier. All movies, magazines, TV programs, and physical surroundings on the premises were from the former era. At the end of the experiment, most of the men showed measurable improvement in memory, sight, and physical strength just by revisiting an earlier time in their life. The younger mindset had reduced their dependence on medical devices and facilitated an overall mental and physical transformation. Dr. Langer believes that "mindset manipulation" can counteract presumed physiological limits, reverse aging, and possibly eradicate many health conditions. Ongoing research by Doctor Joe Dispenza and Scientist David Sinclair have exponentially expanded the field of knowledge on age reversal and self-healing. Their breakthrough studies have demonstrated scientifically that we have enormous capacity to modify our current status and significantly elevate our mental, physical, emotional and spiritual well-being.

We are all conditioned to believe that we need to act and assume the role of the older person as we age, especially after the age of 50. Preordained behavior becomes our daily routine because we are taught that this is how we are supposed to act. But why? Who started this? Refuse to accept it! It's time to write your own script. Untie the ropes anchoring you to someone else's dock. Live intentionally. You decide how you're supposed to live and act. Those who have made the greatest impact on humanity have always been the men and women who refused to comply with a tradition that didn't fit their perception of who they wanted to be. Radical, yes, but think of it this way: If you have not accomplished in life what you hoped to accomplish by following traditional beliefs, then those beliefs are not working for you. Move out of your comfort zone. Change your trajectory.

How do you write a new script? It is a present-tense description of who and what you are. It's your mindset. For example: When I am running in the morning, I repeat several times, to the rhythm of my gait, a simple saying intended to convey a feeling of control over my circumstances and my general outlook on life. *"I am happy, healthy, young, and wealthy."* Here's what it means to me:

- **Happy.** Happiness is a learned habit. It is the understanding that just being alive is a joyful experience. Every day provides opportunities to smile and be grateful. The "Someday I'll" crowd will never be happy. These are the individuals who say, "When I get that better job, then I'll be happy" or "As soon as I pay off my mortgage, I'll be happy. When I meet the right person, lose this extra weight, or have a million dollars in my bank account, then I'll be happy." Even if you realize all of these accomplishments and more, you will not be happy. You just think you will. You must learn how to be contented and appreciate the here and now, not the someday-I'll-be-happy way of life. The present is the only time that happiness can be experienced. Don't let another day pass waiting for happiness to miraculously appear. Learn how to be happy today.

- **Healthy.** Healthy is also a state of mind. There are some conditions we do not have control over; however, the vast majority of conditions are a result of our own doing. What we eat and drink, our sleeping habits, and our exercise regimens are all within our control. It's difficult at first to make healthy choices, but the end results are well worth the effort. If large amounts of your time are spent watching movies based on dysfunctional social interactions between the characters, looking at porn, engaged in blood-and-guts gaming, and a deluge of other negative influences, how can you possibly cultivate the healthy state of mind needed to bring out your best? I'll answer that question for you: It's impossible. Surround yourself with positive influences. Read good books, listen to motivational recordings, place inspirational artwork and phrases around your physical surroundings, and always associate with people who will bring you up.

- **Young**. Young, in my context, is an all-encompassing description of how I feel and think. New ideas, new associates, or friends, and new experiences keep us all young in mind and body. Youth over 50 may sound like an oxymoron, but it is achievable with the right mindset, just as health consciousness will likely dictate your overall health.

- **Wealthy**. Wealthy, to me, means far more than financial wealth. It is the accumulation of all of the above, plus a variety of additional assets such as family, friends, opportunity, education, appreciation for the arts and sciences, and a willingness to give back more than you have taken. A wealthy life should be defined as a life of fulfillment, based on what you interpret that to be.

This is my current choice for an overall mindset script. I believe that if I'm happy, healthy, young, and wealthy, I can accomplish anything I desire. You may use it or create a mindset script that will motivate and define who you are, even if you are not that person yet. Remember, it must be in the present tense. Through repetition, your subconscious mind will interpret your message as an order and begin actualizing your request. All of your goals will be easier to attain when your mindset script is energizing the rest of your efforts.

William Shakespeare said, *"All the world's a stage, and all the men and women merely players."* We are all on life's stage. Sometimes we play the role of a parent or grandparent, a teacher, doctor, nurse, mechanic, construction worker, or friend. The roles are endless and usually modified in each of our different encounters. My role as a commercial real estate broker was that of a competent, top achiever, providing valuable advice to the elite investors in my market. I enjoyed that role immensely because it fit my personality perfectly. I wasn't that person when I first appeared on that stage, but I became better and better at that script the more capable and educated I became. For many investors, we were the go-to brokers for their larger transactions. From day one, we positioned our agency to provide a level of service unrivaled in our community. We succeeded and were rewarded appropriately. You must develop your script and the mindset necessary to be successful on the stage you choose. In other words, write it, perform it, and own it.

Staying in the Game

"Anyone can start from now and make a
brand-new ending." —Carl Bard

ONE OF MY REAL ESTATE CLIENTS, Dick M, owned a large earth-moving business in New Hampshire. His type of company is first on a site to prepare the roads and parking fields, install utilities, and level the dirt for building. He specialized in large-scale commercial projects such as major shopping centers.

During the early '90s real estate meltdown in New Hampshire, when most of our banks failed, Dick was forced to file for bankruptcy due to non-payment by three regional developers who owed his company large sums of money. They, too, were handcuffed with several unoccupied properties, meaning they had no rental income or sales to honor their contracts. Once Dick's company did their work, there was nothing to repossess. It was a devastating event for him and his family. Most of his equipment and his headquarters were auctioned off at pennies on a dollar. He was forced to start over over 50. But what could he do? He knew the earth-moving business, but with little money and most of his equipment gone, how could he orchestrate a comeback? This is when taking time to determine what makes you unique makes all the difference.

A few years later, our town started experiencing rapid population growth. New neighborhoods were being approved almost monthly. Dick decided that, instead of being at the mercy of developers, he would become the developer. He had worked with developers most of his career and had a thorough understanding of their function. He was able to partner with a local investor to buy land and develop his own residential subdivisions. Once approved, he would then sell the lots either to custom home builders or individuals, depending on market conditions. He rented the equipment needed for the road construction and operated the machines himself until he could afford to hire outside operators and acquire his own equipment again. He retained our firm as brokers to market his lots to the better builders in our community. It didn't take long for him to develop more than 100 premium house lots and several commercial projects, including one of the largest developments on Lake Winnipe-saukee, New Hampshire's premier resort destination. Today, his company owns and manages a prestigious marina on the lake and is responsible for the construction of hundreds of waterfront condominiums. He has come back far more than 100%. Easy, no; successful, yes! I have never met anyone with more belief in his capabilities and the tenacity to finish the job than Dick. He refused to become a victim of the circumstances he inherited.

Houston, We Have a Problem

If one story embodies the understanding of the Essential Common Denominators of Success in practical terms, it's that of Jim Lovell, the captain of Apollo 13. In high school, he wanted to be an engineer working on rockets, an entirely new field at the time. His second choice was to be an aviator in the Navy. With high school graduation nearing, he decided to pursue his two-career paths. After talking to the head of the American Rocket Society, he realized that the education he needed to become a rocket engineer was too costly for his family to subsidize. They were barely getting by managing life's essentials. His second choice was also a no-go because the only way to achieve his goal of becoming a Navy pilot would be a commission at the Naval Academy. There wasn't any room for him there. Both doors were closed.

However, as Jim puts it, "A new door opened. It wasn't planned, but there it was, a start-up program from the Navy." This program allowed him to attend a local Wisconsin

college, paid for by the Navy, with the promise of a commission if he passed the grades and was physically capable of
piloting an aircraft. He graduated, and his goal of becoming
a Navy pilot became a reality.

Shortly after graduation from the academy, he was on
a training mission in the South Pacific. He was required to
take off and land on one of the Navy's aircraft carriers, the
Shangri-La, patrolling in the Sea of Japan. The mission required that the carrier be in total darkness. He took off and
preceded with the mission; however, something didn't seem
right with the course he was following, so he contacted the
ship. The ship's radar was not working, and the crew couldn't
locate where he was. Jim determined that he was heading
straight to a city in Japan because it had approximately the
same heading that he had entered into his location finder.
To read the maps, Jim plugged a light into the plane's power
system, but unfortunately, that effort shorted out all of the
aircraft's electrical lighting components. This meant that
there was no assurance that his instruments were accurate
and no lights to display the readings. He was flying in total
darkness with no options but to consider ditching the plane
in the ocean when his fuel ran out, even though the chance
of a rescue at sea was nearly impossible. Landing on the
carrier was equally perilous; without an altimeter and with
the ship in darkness, he could be either too high or too low
for a landing and potentially slam into the rear of the ship,

assuming he could locate it at all. It was a near hopeless situation.

Suddenly, on the horizon, Lovell could see very faint phosphorus light in the darkness. He immediately determined from his extensive training that he was observing planktonic algae being churned up from the bottom of the sea by the Shangri-La's giant impellers, providing what looked like a green runway right to the back of the dark ship. The closer he got, the brighter the luminescence. If the lights in the plane had not shorted out, this singular path to a successful landing that night would not have been visible.

Years later, when Apollo 13 encountered a near-catastrophic event, no doubt his experience from that night of darkness helped Captain Lovell administer the situation with the confidence and focus that helped save himself and the two other astronauts in the space module. Who can forget, "Houston, we have a problem!" Jim says it took thousands of team members who were innovative, motivated, and determined to bring the occupants of Apollo 13 back to Earth. It was crisis management at the highest level. Odds were certainly against a successful conclusion to the failed mission more than 200,000 miles from home. As captain, Jim accepted responsibility for the outcome. He focused on possibilities and adapted to the changes taking place to cope with the emergency. He relied on his unique accumulated knowledge and training to guide him and his crew. He had faith in his team in Houston and the belief that they could administrate a successful recovery. When splashdown occurred and the capsule door opened with all three occupants alive, the entire world breathed a sigh of relief.

Another Green Jacket

Eleven years had passed since Tiger Woods, once the world's most formidable golf pro, had won a major tournament. After multiple back and knee surgeries, most of his peers and the sports authorities believed his best days were behind him. His mental game was also significantly impaired from a string of personal setbacks, including a high-profile divorce and an encounter with police while driving under the influence of prescription drugs. Everyone counted Tiger out but Tiger himself. Against all odds, in 2019 he won the biggest golf event on the planet, the Masters Tournament, and regained his status as a top contending pro.

We can learn from his own review of his steps to victory that day that the Essential Common Denominators of Success were clearly in play. He used his unique talents and collective knowledge of the game to provide a base for a comeback. He took complete responsibility for his past reversal of fortune and had the faith and belief that he was capable of future successes. He changed his swing to accommodate the new realities of his physical condition and invested a vast quantity of time focusing on strength training and practice on the golf course to prepare for future events. His goal that year was to win the Masters Tournament, not just compete. When asked about an exceptionally difficult putt he had made during the tournament, he referenced his father's influence by noting, "My dad used to say the putts in the picture." In other words, he visualized the direction of the ball traveling over the terrain and its path into the hole. When asked if he could render any advice to others struggling as he did, he started by saying, "Never, never give up, that's a given."

He is right! Never take yourself out of the game, no matter what the odds. Starting over over 50 will change certain options, but you can adjust and proceed forward. Although Tiger was not 50 at the time of this victory, the process is the same for everyone rebuilding their career or status. Identify what makes you unique and rely on your collective knowledge, set your goals, invest the necessary time training to be successful, visualize the outcome, and have the faith and belief that you can and will accomplish your mission. Tiger did exactly that and look at the result—another green jacket for one of the greatest comebacks in sports history. Just four weeks later, he was the recipient of a Medal of Freedom citation, the nation's highest civilian award. If he had accepted defeat and the status quo, he would never have realized his greatest victory or his return to the success and status he once held. He chose winning over reminiscing.

The Worst Possible Choice

All of us get discouraged from time to time. What you don't want to do is allow those feelings to continue for a protracted period of time. It will only make the situation much worse. Remember, thoughts are powerful messages. We want to send positive messages to ourselves, not negative ones. Remember, it is your option to choose what you think about most.

Focusing only on the negative in difficult situations can produce catastrophic results. Clyde, a very successful owner of multifamily properties, stopped at our office to discuss replacing his apartments with less management-intensive commercial properties such as office buildings or retail centers. He communicated to us that he had been working for more than 20 years managing his portfolio of small apartments. He built equity by doing most of the work himself. He became the painter, the plumber, the electrician, the carpenter, and the collector of rents. Basically, he was a one-man show. With the number of units under his control, it was not uncommon for him to work seventy-hour weeks quite often. His business was not much different from my talent agency business, labor-intensive and with little time off. Nights, days, weekends, and holidays were all working days.

At the time we met, Clyde had just sold all his residential properties and now had more than $5 million to reinvest in what he hoped would be a major step up in the quality of his life. We presented shopping centers and office buildings within our market that provided the income and relief he sought. Clyde, however, was also communicating with a financial advisor who convinced him that the booming economy in Florida would enhance his income and accelerate his property values far greater than investing in the more mature New Hampshire market.

Along with one of my top brokers, I traveled to Florida to view these opportunities firsthand. After spending two days touring the investments, we were both of the same opinion. It may be possible to achieve the results being projected but only if everything were to go perfectly. Cost overruns during construction, longer vacancy periods, competitors, and potential tenant turnovers could present significant problems in an emerging market. Nevertheless, Clyde decided to go forward with the Florida projects despite our recommendation that he reconsider that decision.

A few years later, the country was experiencing a mild recession; however, in his part of Florida it was a major recession. Clyde had invested all of his own money and had initiated several bank loans to finance numerous additional properties. Everything he had worked for evaporated very quickly because of the rapid slowdown of new tenants and the failure of many of his existing tenants. He was broke and facing foreclosure on all his properties. On a weekend visit back to New Hampshire, he committed suicide. I'm certain that he took his own life in part because he couldn't accept the outcome that everything he had accumulated was gone, and the prospect of starting over over 50 was too overwhelming to consider.

It is such a sad ending because Clyde had the capability and the unique knowledge needed to rebuild his net worth. I know this would have been possible for him because some of our brokerage clients who had filed for bankruptcy at one point in their career later became some of our largest investors. Negative thoughts of "no way out" must have permeated Clyde's thinking, and he chose to end his timeline prematurely. He made the worst possible choice. Never let thoughts of hopelessness and despair overwhelm rational thought. If it's only money, remember that the world is full of money and it can be replaced. Life is priceless. It cannot be replaced.

CHAPTER

31

TIME FOR ACTION

"I have been impressed with the urgency of doing.
Knowing is not enough; we must apply.
Being willing is not enough; we must do."
—Leonardo Da Vinci

THE QUESTION YOU SHOULD be asking yourself right now is, "What specialized knowledge do I have that can be of value to others and help me acquire the success and happiness I desire?" All of us have valuable skills. Just as my search for a path to success led me to a career in commercial real estate, your search will also lead you to an obvious choice. You are never without options. Even your current or previous career can be reinvented the same way an old song is brought back with a present-day musical style, becoming a hit all over again. Your hit could be an assimilation of all your experiences or the new venture you dreamed of pursuing at some point. This may be that point. You will never be any younger. Don't undermine your options by looking at the obstacles you are now facing. What you don't have right now doesn't really matter. Focus instead on the possibilities and set your goals accordingly.

The Box

When our family was forced to sell our McMansion, we were all under significant stress. One night, during the process of sorting through and packing our household inventory for the pending moving date, Carol finally succumbed to the pressure. There were at least 20 boxes packed and we had hardly dented the years of accumulated stuff when Carol, half crying, half screaming blurted out, *"Next time we move, everyone will get only ONE BOX...THAT'S IT...ONE BOX!"*

After venting her frustration with the situation, she decided to retire for the evening. I put my daughter Kristi to bed and joined Carol for a much-needed rest. The next morning, I went into Kristi's room to see how she was making out. Every stuffed animal she had ever accumulated was on display. She had them lined up five deep on her bed and two deep on the shelves of her bookcase. She was sitting on her window seat with a few of her favorites in her lap and staring at the rest of her collection. Without looking away from her treasures, she asked, "Daddy, how big is the box?"

I knew precisely what she was referring to. I joined her on

the window seat, put my arm around her, and then assured her, "As big as it needs to be, to put all of your guys in it."

I couldn't forget this incident. It surprised me that my seven-year-old daughter was already focusing on solutions to what must have been an overwhelming concern for her. At that time, my own problems seemed so devastating that thinking in terms of solutions was not even on my radar screen yet.

Starting over over 50, or any age for that matter, requires immediate action, not excuses. Don't wait for a better time. The journey of a thousand miles really does begin with a single step. Take that first step right now. List your experiences and the areas about which you are knowledgeable. Make the box as big as it needs to be. Don't limit your possibilities by eliminating choices because of age, assets, or other perceived roadblocks. At this point, make it unlimited. I was surprised to learn that normal human vision can pick out a candle burning more than a mile away. (My guess would have been less than a tenth of that distance.) Similarly, don't limit your thinking because of a perception you have become attached to.

Kristi now has a lap dog named Kaptain. When she returns home for a visit, he becomes my grand-doggie, ready for a walk around the old neighborhood. One of his particular traits is that he intimidates larger dogs when we encounter them on his route. Not just any dog, but the biggest dogs! I have to hold the leash very tight to keep him from attacking the other dog. What is most surprising is that in the majority of encounters the other dog is usually intimidated by Kaptain's aggressiveness and backs off very quickly or tries to run away from him. Jokingly, I suggested that my daughter should buy him a mirror for Christmas.

Our self-image is no different. The bigger dogs could eat Kaptain for a snack, but they don't realize that. We all have the capacity to achieve far greater victories than we do; however, our self-image dictates otherwise. A hunk of coal and the world's most valuable diamonds share the same DNA. This is why believing in yourself and your capabilities is so important. You can never achieve more than you think you can achieve. Comparing your success to someone else's success will always leave you frustrated and envious. Both emotions are counterproductive. What is important is that you propagate the assets you have, just as Helen Keller did. At five-foot-seven I'll never compete with Michael Jordan in a slam-dunk contest, but I am certain my knowledge of investment real estate is far superior to his knowledge of that subject.

If you have been successful in the past, you are more than capable of regaining that status. It is extremely important that you do not hide from your family, friends, or associates. You will need their support to regain your footing. A prisoner is placed in solitary confinement as punishment.

Don't lock yourself in an imaginary prison. I placed myself in that prison after my meltdown and delayed my own recovery by more than three years. It was a major mistake. Many spend decades in that prison, and some never leave. The more normal your daily activities, the quicker you can begin to rebuild all of your mental, emotional, spiritual, social, and financial assets.

Earlier I noted that some acquaintances acted as if my financial condition was contagious. This was pointed out to make you aware that it's not uncommon to encounter this type of reaction from a few people. Ignore them. Failure is just an event. You are still the same person you have always been. Your character shouldn't change with the balance in your bank account. You may have had a financial failure, but you are not a failed person. The most important critic is you. Never diminish your value or self-esteem based on someone else's opinion of who you are. As Eleanor Roosevelt once remarked, "No one can make you feel inferior without your consent."

It is easy to be intimidated by others or to assume they know more than you do when you are going through a rebuilding process. You're wounded and vulnerable to criticism, but don't allow it to enter your conscious mind and distract you from your mission. It's only your perception of the situation that causes so much pain. A doctor friend of mine related a story of how he felt on a recent tour of notable wineries in the Sonoma and Napa Valley areas of California. At one of the tastings, the vintner asked each of the participants to describe the wine they were drinking. The first person asked to respond was sampling the winery's red zinfandel. He said it had a rich ruby color with a bouquet that hints of raspberry, plum, and black cherry, with a chocolatey finish that seemed to linger indefinitely. The second person described her chardonnay as a golden glass of sunshine with a crisp but engaging finish, harboring subtle nuances of pear, mango, honeydew, and grapefruit. Realizing he could not compete with the eloquent narratives just presented but refusing to be intimidated by them either, the doctor simply said his glass of wine tasted like "crushed grapes." Arguably, his simple answer could not be challenged. Although he is a recognized authority on intricate heart procedures, the only knowledge he has of wine is what he likes. Act as the doctor did! Refuse to be intimidated by anyone or by any of the circumstances you will encounter. If some individuals or groups make you uncomfortable, avoid them. Trust yourself and the pieces will fall into place.

OPK

If you're over 50, you may not have grown up during the technical revolution, but you're certainly a part of it now. This revolution has created unprecedented opportunities for those with creative ideas and the ambition to start a new undertaking. Peter Drucker once said, *"A business will survive only as long as it can afford to pay for its mistakes."* Without money, the survival of any business or individual effort is short-lived. In the past, the time it took to establish a new business or professional services firm was usually five years or more, due to the inherent learning curve that businesses large and small must go through before the fundamental success techniques could be developed. This is why so many business and personal endeavors failed—the money ran out. However, one of the greatest advancements in human history has occurred over the last few decades and continues to accelerate on a daily basis. Most of the accumulated knowledge of all humanity is only a few clicks away. We now have access to information that can transform the life of any business or individual. What once took years to learn can now be acquired in a fraction of that time. We've all heard the expression OPM, meaning "other people's money," but there is something far more valuable—OPK, "other people's knowledge," often defined as the new currency.

When we started our commercial real estate agency, one of the most difficult tasks was determining who would be our clients. That's easy to see in residential real estate since everyone needs a place to live, but only a limited number of prospects have a requirement for commercial property. During the first few years, most of the leads were garnered from trade journals. They usually reported who was buying and selling commercial real estate. Tracking down the contact information of those individuals was a very time-consuming task, which generally required traveling to county registries and town halls to learn the identity behind the LLC or corporate entity. Only the largest agencies, with enormous assets, could develop the databases necessary to provide a supply of quality leads to their agents in the field. Small agencies had no other choice but to literally knock on doors or invest in expensive advertising, hoping to identify a client. However, a few years into the business, things began to change exponentially. Internet databases, online listing capabilities, and timely news flashes provided instant information about clients and their needs. Access that was available only to the elite group of star performers in our industry became available to everyone. For the first time in history, small agencies could compete on a level playing field with these giants. Information that could have taken five to 10 years to accumulate was now available on demand.

OPK can arm almost any individual or business with the fundamental knowledge needed to establish, compete, and thrive in any undertaking. It is not a magic bullet but a resource that can eliminate years of trial and error efforts. This is significant since time is our most valuable asset. The music business was formerly dominated by record companies that controlled virtually all facets of the industry. Today, a recording done on a laptop computer and listed with any of the music services can potentially become an international hit. Online college courses and specialty training is available to everyone. Once you determine what you are most qualified or most interested in pursuing, there is a wealth of information at your fingertips to help you make the right choices. When you review the experiences and procedures from several companies or individuals with expertise in your field, their best practices will become apparent. Avoid common mistakes and focus on the common winning strategies. For example, the most successful commercial real estate firms generally use professional database services to blast emails to thousands of potential clients rather than rely exclusively on their own lists. They attend trade shows to meet with prospects in person. They provide current market data to assist their clients in making proper decisions and most will attend seminars learning the latest innovations in property utilization, financial structures, and what's moving the markets in general. Most specialize in a specific property type such as retail or medical office rather than a general practitioner. They become experts in their specialty.

You can achieve more in less time today than at any other time in history. Skip a few games or movies and invest the time in yourself. Live your dreams instead of watching other people live theirs. Technology can help you get there, but you need a plan and the desire to make it happen. For example, during the COVID-19 lock-down, many people with specialized knowledge offered on-line courses to create income and help others looking to learn more about their particular field. There are always options available to you when you look for them.

It may begin to sound redundant, but an obvious path will become apparent if you do your homework and begin writing down possibilities and the steps necessary to accomplish your goals. It's so simple, and it has worked for many others in similar circumstances. It has worked for me—using the same instructions you are receiving. Start by writing a few sentences and watch how quickly they become paragraphs of opportunity. Use visualization boards that you can review daily and have faith in yourself and your mission. This is not a difficult process; anyone can do it. You just need to begin. It's always scary to let go of our familiar past or move out of our comfort zone and start down an unknown path, but no sunrise can light our way without relinquishing the night. As Martin Luther King, Jr said, *"Take the first step in faith. You don't need to see the whole staircase."*

ILLUSTRATING YOUR GOALS

"Your goals are the road maps that guide you
and show you what's possible in your life."
—Les Brown

ONCE YOU HAVE DETERMINED what you are uniquely qualified to do, you need to establish realistic goals and a plan for achieving them. Time and time again, study after study has proven the validity of written goals. A comprehensive study that was initiated by a major university determined that 10 years after graduation, students who had written goals and a clear vision of their future were considerably more successful than their counterparts who did not have established written goals. Definitive, written goals will help you make much better choices and minimize wasted time and energy. We all know this! If you're over 50, you have heard it a thousand times. You know it works.

There are literally dozens of new books every year that discuss methods of goal-setting. It doesn't need to be anything more than a single sheet of paper that clearly defines what you intend to do and a plan of action. That's really it! You don't need hundreds of pages to properly set your goals. Sometimes less is more. Look at your list repetitively, several times a day, until you have programmed it into your subconscious mind. It is impossible not to move in the direction of your thoughts. Think small, you will stay small. Think you are beaten, you are beaten. Think you are not worthy; you are not worthy. Think of ill health and you will be at the doctor's office repeatedly. Think success, not failure. Think of winning, not stagnation. Think happiness and joy and then opportunities will present themselves.

The hardest battle you will ever encounter is the one between your ears. It takes discipline to win it, but you have the power to do just that. You are in complete control of your thoughts. You may not be able to control every event that you encounter, but you do have control over how you react and your attitude toward situations beyond your control. The good news is that you are in control of the vast majority of circumstances that happen in your life. Win this battle and you are well on your way back to success, or to achieving the success you always wanted.

Desire

One of Carol's favorite summertime destinations was Ogunquit, Maine, a small coastal village. It features a dramatic hillside pathway over the rocky terrain, providing commanding views of the Atlantic Ocean. The last time we hiked that path, Carol became short of breath and needed to rest on one of the observation benches. While we were there, I noticed two sailboats about a quarter-mile from shore traveling in opposite directions, though they were both navigating by the same winds. Those winds are similar to the power of desire, which can propel you forward to any destination or goal when you know where you want to go.

Unrelenting desire is paramount to achieving your goals and not succumbing to other distractions, such as the comfort of excuses or doing nothing and chilling out instead of improving and executing your plan. In other words, you have to really want to win if you expect to win. Wishing and hoping just won't cut it. The old saying "When the going gets tough, the tough get going" is appropriate in this context. Don't settle for mediocrity when things get difficult by lowering your expectations and compromising your destiny. We are all gifted with seeds of greatness, but they need that fire from within to make them grow. Once the fire is started, you are the only person who can extinguish the blaze. How is it started? By first believing you are on a mission that only you can complete. There is no turning back. You're in it to win it, no matter what it takes.

If you feel tired and lacking in energy, look at your diet, sleep schedule, and exercise routine. Are you willing to improve these areas of your life? If you smoke or drink too much alcohol, are you willing to exchange those habits for healthy alternatives? These types of choices may be painful but doing nothing will be much more painful in the long run.

Deep-rooted desire is almost impossible to stop. Don't allow those around you, no matter how well-intentioned, to discourage you from your efforts. If they say it's impossible, it probably is for them—but not for you. You will be tested every step along the way, but an unyielding desire and reasonable discipline will place you in the winner's circle where you belong.

Tom Brady is one of the most successful quarterbacks in NFL history. His desire to win is so strong that he has accomplished what has been termed "impossible" even by his critics. He spends 80 hours a week preparing for a one-hour game. One of his teammates once declared that "Brady's desire to win is so strong that he is literally the first person in the room viewing tapes and strategy, and at the end of the session, the person who turns off the lights." He works on the practice field every day as if he were a rookie trying to impress the coach. As he ages, he relies more on his mental ability to know what the other 21 players on the field will do on almost every play. This is the benefit of age and experience. What he may lack in physical ability is more than compensated for by his mental toughness and desire to win. His success didn't happen by chilling out, investing hours on social media, or watching reruns of his favorite sitcom. It happened because of his unrelenting desire to win. Follow his regimen and it will be impossible for you to fail.

As you formalize your goals, they should include career planning, finances, fun, relationships, personal development, health, and education. Most can consist of a few sentences under each heading, with the exception of rebuilding your career and finances. These will require a more comprehensive approach because your unique skills will dictate the scope of your written plans. Be specific. For example, under your health goals, indicate what your daily routine will be. Awake at 6:30 a.m. Listen to at least seven minutes of positive music or messages before any other activity. Run three miles every other day with yoga and weights alternating on the off days. Under diet, list the right combination of foods to propagate a healthy physiological system. Under education, how much time will you commit to reading specific periodicals or listening to podcasts that will improve your knowledge base and provide a greater opportunity for success and advancement in your career? Under finances, develop an actual budget to control your resources and expectations of future income from your endeavors. If you need an investor, this is where you make plans for the amounts anticipated and a strategy to locate this type of funding. Include a timeline for every category and organize your plan of action. Simply stated: What do I want to do? When am I going to do it? How am I going to do it? And finally, am I really committed and willing to do what is necessary to change my life?

I am deliberately making this easy for you because so much has been reported about goal-setting that it's intimidating to many people. It is a wasted effort if the goals are too complex and time-consuming to be of any real value. How hard can it be to write a couple of sentences in your notebook or tablet and start listing your dreams and options? That's how it all begins. It's not complicated. It really is that simple! Every dream fulfilled and every successful venture begins with basic ideas that evolve into a plan of action. Once you begin, you will feel the excitement and power that comes from knowing where you are headed. We humans have enormous stores of energy when we are on a mission. You will amaze yourself, just as I amazed myself, at what can be achieved with nothing more than simple ideas written down and the will to act on those ideas.

- Simple is good!

- Simple with a plan of action is better!

- Simple with a plan of action initiated today is best!

Don't procrastinate; start writing down your goals. As the Nike slogan commands, "Just do it!" No one else can do it for you.

SUCCESS AND HAPPINESS

REMEMBER THIS! No one has ever lived in the future, and therefore it is infinitely changeable. How exciting is that! The start of each new day is a level playing field for all of us. That field is both in our minds and the physical world. Napoleon once said, *"Imagination rules the world."* One idea or new opportunity acted on today can transform all your tomorrows. Think of the many men and women whose first great idea or opportunity came to them when they were over 50, people who late in life acquired fortune, fame, and happiness beyond their wildest dreams. It's happening more now than at any other time in history due to the resources provided by social media and internet marketing. It's worth repeating. Every new day provides endless possibilities. Stay calm under pressure. Purge negative thoughts and replace them with visualizations of what you want. It is within your power to make that choice. Choose to live the life you desire.

Believe you are worthy. Expect good things to happen and they will begin to happen.

We all have considerably more capacity than we use. Many neurologists believe that an average brain has over 100 billion neurons. That is a massive amount of human computing power that is accessible to us 24/7. Everything you need, you already possess. Dick M could look at a pile of rocks and see an artistically designed stone wall. That is exactly how the components of your experiences materialize. When pieced together, they are the formidable assets that only you possess. You are a one-of-one original. Be proud of your credentials and press forward with your head up.

Wherever your road takes you, pursue it with relentless passion. It doesn't matter how many times you may have failed in the past, today is a new day. Without some forms of failure, success wouldn't be possible. Have you ever watched a baby learn to walk? The baby will continue trying, and the parents will keep encouraging, until the baby is on two feet. Why, because we know it's possible to walk on two feet. The process for attaining success and happiness is identical. No one can walk for us. They can help us, encourage us, teach us, pray for us, but they cannot walk for us. You have to do it.

We are all subject to the Essential Common Denominators of Success. Review them every day. Any time you begin to feel discouraged, read them again and again to assure yourself that success and happiness is within reach.

Don't let the imaginary fears and undesirable habits of your past regain control and cause you to stagnate. Over the last one hundred years or so, many philosophers and psychologists have been able to identify and validate these Essential Common Denominators of Success with precision accuracy. How do we know they are accurate? We know because they apply to everyone and have the same result over and over again when common criteria are inputted.

The Edge

There are only slight differences between most people, but those little differences make all the difference. Consider Las Vegas casinos. They have a slight edge on winning, and yet that small percentage produces billions and billions of dollars a year for building and operating the finest casinos and hotels in the world. You can make the odds work for you by just doing a little more than your comfort level encourages you to do. Start every morning with some form of positive stimulus from your personal library of motivational resources, including uplifting music or reading material that will set the tone for the day. Compile a list of your favorite quotes that inspire and motivate you. They are a powerful reinforcement tool. Online sites that offer a daily positive message are also beneficial. Stay away from social media, TV, newspapers, or radio news until you have a minimum seven to 10 minutes of positive programming. The whole world isn't going to change in seven to 10 minutes, and it will strengthen your resolve to sustain your progress regardless of the "noise" around you. Do this for at least 28 days and you will never go back to your old routine. This small investment initiates the slight edge you will need at the start of every day. This is the time to focus on thoughts of success, happiness, wellness, family, friendships, and reviewing your plans for the day. Combining physical exercise with this program every morning will significantly compound your edge.

Keep the end game in mind. It is considerably better to take action than to pay the consequences of a reaction. Wouldn't it be the preferred choice to leave before a tidal wave rather than try to swim in one? Take the first step by organizing your plans, creating your visualization boards, and starting to implement those plans immediately. As Winston Churchill once said, "Perfection is the enemy of progress." Even a bad plan that is acted on is a thousand times better than a great plan that is idle. Wayne Gretzky, Hall of Fame hockey legend, puts it this way: "You miss 100% of the shots you don't take." Remember, your timeline runs concurrently with your choice line. Time eliminates choice, which is why you must act on your plans immediately. They can be modified or enhanced as more pertinent data emerges.

It seems so simple, yet the vast majority of people who want to better themselves never invest the amount of time they spend watching a movie to consider how to improve their lives. They essentially allow the flow of the day to randomly determine the outcome of that day. Don't do that! Control your time and invest it in worthwhile pursuits. Turn off the TV, shut down the distractions and tell your body to sit down, right here, right now and don't even consider getting up until you have a written outline to "your" story. When you know where you want to go, it is amazing how much you can accomplish, and in much less time than you ever thought possible. Studies have determined that less than 5 percent of the population has written goals. How is that possible, especially when the same research confirms that individuals with written goals accomplish infinitely more than those individuals without written goals? Do not cheat on this step—write down your goals and plans. It is the bridge to accomplishment. It's the difference between the doers and the dreamers, winning or regretting.

My return to success started with a thorough review and implementation of the fundamentals presented here. Starting is the hardest decision. It's uncomfortable, and it is work, but once you're on your way it becomes considerably easier. Success came to me at the expense of a great failure. Would I do it all over again? Yes, I would! I am so grateful that I had the opportunity, and the desire, to administrate a recovery that exceeded far more than I had envisioned on my awakening night. The journey has educated me, challenged me, and on occasion frustrated me, but I wouldn't trade this adventure for any sum of money or the comfort of a passive existence. Experience is the severest, but certainly the best teacher.

It's not too late to regain the life you once enjoyed or to create the life you have imagined. You are not alone in your efforts. You have plenty of company. There is a verse from one of Barry Manilow's songs that reinforces that point of view:

> *I made it through the rain*
> *And found myself respected*
> *By the others who*
> *Got rained on too.*
> *And made it through...*

It is our responsibility to live well and finish well. We know this is not a dress rehearsal. Today is the only day you have to make a difference in your life. Make it count! Kill the excuses, get to work, and join in with all the others who, got rained on too, and made it through. There is no plan B. No plan B. No...

Epilogue:
Plan A

1. Purchase a journal or a spiral notebook that you can carry with you everywhere you go. This is mandatory. Use it to memorialize your thoughts on any given day. You don't want to lose your best ideas because you can't remember them. Open your journal and write a list of every job you have ever held and include the activities you enjoy, and are proficient enough that they could be of value to others. Do not worry about money. Think in terms of what you can contribute first, and the money will follow. You will be paid in direct proportion to the value that you bring to society.

2. Study the list until an obvious utilization or combination of these skills and experiences becomes apparent. Quiet meditation usually produces an effective result. It may require a few sessions to be in the zone, but if you are persistent and demand an answer, an answer will surface.

3. Start writing down every random thought that comes to mind during your quiet times, without any restrictions. From those random thoughts, create a cohesive plan of attack by putting first things first. This is your initial rough draft back to success.

4. What additional specialized training or knowledge will be necessary? Where will it come from? Think Other People's Knowledge!

5. What resources do you have and what resources will you need? If you need additional investment capital, what's the plan to acquire that asset? Will it be self-funded, friends, family, bank, or other investors?

6. Finalize the rough draft and start working on each segment by writing down the preliminary goals that need to be accomplished in order to advance to the next step. Keep it simple but write it down.

7. After the initial comeback plan, start writing down goals for financial expectations, personal improvement in health, education, relationships, and don't forget those crazy dreams. Houses, cars, vacations, college tuition, charities, and all the other perks successful people expect from the attainment of their goals.

8. Create visualization boards, electronic or hard copy, for all your expectations. Look at them every day or

as often as needed to keep you on the right track. These are powerful tools to have in your possession.

9. Review the Essential Common Denominators of Success daily to keep you grounded in faith, hope, and belief in your mission.

10. Sharpen your edge every morning with an absolute minimum of seven minutes of positive reinforcement plus a period of physical exercise to prepare your body and mind for the challenges of the day. Write and repeat your overall mindset script several times daily. Commitment and discipline will win out over adversity.

These are the top 10 steps needed to acquire the prosperity you rightfully deserve. Stay focused, follow plan A, and get it done.

AUTHOR BIO

TOM FINI GREW UP IN A HOUSING PROJECT in central Massachusetts. His participation in a teenage rock and roll band led him to a career as a talent agent, record producer and owner of a young adult nightclub facility, providing him significant wealth and success by the age of 40.

Unfortunately, through a series of poor choices and adverse market conditions, he lost everything and accumulated mountains of debt in the process. Tom had to face the realization that he would be "Starting Over...Over 50", with no money, no degree and no obvious resources to begin again.

This book provides a detailed look at his experiences in his search for answers. Filled with inspiring personal stories and his epiphany on rewinding age, Tom provides a roadmap to success that can be navigated by any man or woman over 50, 60, or even 70. He reveals the 10 Essential Common Denominators of Success that apply to everyone seeking achievement and happiness later in life.

Tom now resides in New Hampshire with his family and friends close by.